A KID OF STEEL

Published by ACM Retro Ltd,
The Grange,
Church Street,
Dronfield,
Sheffield S18 1QB.

Visit ACM Retro at:
www.acmretro.con

A catalogue record for this book is available from the British Library.

A KID OF STEEL

SHIRECLIFFE FOR STARTERS, BIRLEY FOR AFTERS

I would like to dedicate this book to the following ladies in my life:

My mother Marie for the past 46 years

My guardian angels: grandma's Florence, Florence Emily, Gertrude and not forgetting auntie Lillian

My wife Christine and daughter Samantha for the constant overwhelming support

My dearly departed mother in law Barbara another one who pointed me in the right direction

And last but not least the greatest dad in the world... James Cronshaw.

Contents

Another Kid on the Shirecliffe Block

As I opened my eyes to the world for the very first time I could hardly focus on my surroundings, where was I?

I'd been safe for the past nine months in my snug and darkened room, and then all of a sudden I was on a helter skelter ride to where I did not know?

I finally emerged into the light with my stinging eyes hardly open, I felt someone grab for my legs and before I knew it everything was topsy turvey, then whack!

I'd taken an almighty direct hit onto my rear end, and boy did I let out a cry to equal all cries, if I could have talked I'd have given my aggressor a piece of my mind, but for the time being I remained speechless.

Next minute they'd taken a sharp pair of scissors to me and the slithering snake that had been attached to yours truly for more than an age was ceremoniously dumped onto a silver tray.

Bloody hell what had it done to them, not even a few minutes in this hostile atmosphere and I had received a great whack on the bottom and poor old snake eyes had well and truly bitten the dust.

Presently, after all the blood and thunder, I'd been taken to another room and was given a very enjoyable scrub down, by this same nurse who had turned from devil to angel in a matter of minutes, this was all very weird, one minute all hell had broken loose and the next, I was being pampered to high heaven!

I had enjoyed my soothing makeover and was now feeling as fresh as a daisy, all cleaned up and nowhere to go.

But wait just a moment, the devil/angel nurse then carried me into another room which was lined with row upon row of beds.

Each one had an occupant who was eyeing me up no end.

Finally I came to rest in the arms of this blonde lady.

This was my mother, Jean, who had carried me for the duration.

Alongside her was a dark haired chap who wore a black suit and looked rather dashing. This was my father, James.

Yes folks, yours truly, Anthony Cronshaw had arrived on the 3rd of November 1955 and boy did it feel good.

I glanced into the mirror hanging on the whitewashed walls and to tell you the truth I was not such a bad looker.

My first resting place was a gigantic wooden cot that was surrounded by wooden bars. There was certainly no escape for this whipper snapper.

I was in the Nether Edge Hospital.

This place was situated in the posh end of Sheffield.

The building used to belong to the Ecclesall Bierlow Workhouse until 1929.

At that time it was home to the poor and destitute who had no-one to care for them or were just down on their luck.

What happened to these wretched people when their home of sorts had to make way for this new hospital with its Gynaecology department is anybody's guess.

Also that was not really something which concerned me at the time, what with me being new born.

I remained in this establishment for, well, I can't really remember how long.

Maybe it was a day or so, but who cared, I bloody loved it.

One morning though it was time to go, and a nice shiny ambulance was commissioned to take me home.

But where was I heading?

Would I be staying locally in these exclusive, tree lined streets of Nether Edge, or some other highly sought after area of this great city?

My transport home came courtesy of the Sheffield Ambulance Service and the livery was the same colour as that of the Transport Department.

We made our way into the city along Abbeydale Road and boy did these houses look the business.

We crossed the River Don at Lady's Bridge and headed through the Wicker with its famous Arches.

Steadily we climbed Spital Hill and the much sought after area of Burngreave with the mansion-like abodes which lined either side of the road.

But my transport trudged on and on before finally it turned into Cookswood Road, a road which seemed to climb to the stars.

These houses looked the business with their imposing bay windows. Yep, a house like this would suit me down to the ground.

Except that we then, started to descend towards Herries Road, before veering into Musgrave Road.

I believed the driver was taking a short cut to the Loxley Valley and the countryside beyond.

I was going to live on a farm and be made for life!

I mean, when was the last time you saw a destitute farmer?

God, my mind was racing and I was thinking that I was only one step away from royalty!

The driver brought our vehicle to a sudden stop and within seconds the doors were flung open and a nurse helped my mother down the steps.

The nurse then handed me over and it was a good job I had been swaddled in my blue shawl because it was freezing.

So, this was it, 20 Musgrave Road.

This was to be my home sweet home.

There to greet me was my Grandma Florence on my mother's side and her husband, William.

Florence had resided on the nearby Southey estate, where her relatives the Marriott's had set up home, after moving from those back to back houses that littered the valley along Penistone Road.

William and Florence Horsman had wed in 1933.

My mother Jean had been born the same year and was the eldest of four children.

They already had three teenage boys also sharing the family home, William Jnr, a strapping 19 year old; Frederick aged 14 and Michael who was the baby of the family at the tender age of 10.

How were we all going to fit into this house?

Had it got expanding walls?

After I'd been manhandled by most of the neighbours, (which included Auntie Lillian and Uncle Frank Guest who lived down the road at number 3) I was eventually allowed to take a rest in my bedroom (it transpired I would actually be sharing with my parents!) I did not want to appear ungrateful, but eight people in a house that shared its grounds with three more houses?

The house was sadly not semi-detached, but at least it was not one of those terraced properties that had no inside toilet or bath.

It was going to be a tight fit, if this little lion was going to get any sleep tonight.

Although the front room was very homely with its roaring fire, the kitchen was tiny.

We would just have to get a shift rota going at mealtimes.

At least the toilet was inside and not at the bottom of the garden.

The coalhouse looked interesting and I envisaged that being a children's playground.

Upstairs we had a bathroom so no tin bath in front of the fire for us. Grandma and Granddad had the master bedroom, while we had the middle sized one while the lads were in the matchbox room; boy did they draw the short straw.

I was placed carefully in a smaller version of my very first sleeping area which I had enjoyed so much during my short stay in the hospital.

I was hoping and praying that my father didn't snore or I'd be dead to the world come the morning.

What I do remember was my bloody nappy was the size of your standard modern day beach towel, and those safety pins were about a foot long.

Well, I survived the night and while I was a contented child as I lay there suckling on my mother's breast, I could feel an icy gust of wind every time one of the lads opened the back door.

You see William Snr had already left for work.

He maintained the tracks on the railways, which helped to keep the trains running safely.

So it was down to Florence to get the roaring fire going every morning, so that the lads could have a nice warm breakfast before they headed for school.

William Jnr was in the building industry, and my father, who worked at Hadfield's in the local steel industry, had also left for their respective jobs; the front room was now feeling a little less cramped and a little more comfortable for the time being.

It was November, the middle of winter, so if you happened to move a couple of feet away from the fire, you would certainly cop for what felt like an arctic blast.

The fire was now blazing away and I watched intently as the two youngest kids were drawn to it like it had a magical spell!

Even though they were old enough to fend for themselves they enjoyed this early morning ritual.

They were grasping mugs of piping hot tea, while their mother - my Gran - impaled slice after slice of thick crusty bread onto this over-sized three pronged fork, which she held dangerously close to the raging fire.

Once that glorious bread that gave off such a beautiful odour had turned a lovely golden brown, lashings of butter would be lovingly spread all over it.

You could see the melted butter drip, drip, and drip some more onto the glowing embers. And it smelled good.

This ritual would be repeated on a daily basis.

Unfortunately I was never included in this early morning family get together, but then neither was my father, Granddad or William Junior.

I was a bonny little bugger and I seemed to be getting bigger by the day.

I had now progressed from the breast, only to be hugely disappointed with the powdered substitute, which tasted truly horrible!

Things started to improve a little when I acquired my first mode of transport; it had four massive wheels, shiny black body work and a hood to die for.

It was a kind of convertible because at the first sign of rain the massive hood would be up like a shot.

Notice that cheeky grin, beaming out for all to see.

How sleek that pram was, I bet it was the best one around the estate.

I would love being taken out in it with my mother and father. We would walk, or at least they would, to the local park in Hillsborough and I loved to watch them feed the ducks.

My mother had to return to work as a clippie for the Transport Department, so it was left to the inseparable and formidable duo of Grandma Florence and Auntie Lillian to care for me.

But to me they were just fondly known as Flo and Lily.

They would parade yours truly around the streets of Shirecliffe and beyond.

My two chaperones would time it to a tee, just passing the Five Arches public house before it closed its doors at 3pm and manage a swift half!

I'd be sat there in my pram and being of such a tender age, the partaking of even a bag of crisps or a bottle of pop was out of the equation.

They were brilliant company and I must have spent most of the time hanging around with these two ladies, the pavements of the area were ours, my pram never ever gave way to no man and even the traffic came to a sudden stop when these girls needed to cross the road, even though to passers-by these two ladies looked daunting I knew from day one I was in safe hands.

People were rushing about, they were gearing themselves up for the visit of Father Christmas, and I was only coming to terms with this way of life, as I marvelled at these soot covered blokes who were busy touting for business.

They offered to clean the chimneys for a price, but there were not many takers around the area, many preferred the good old do it yourself job, they would be better off heading for the posh estates where money was no object.

The festive period passed me by, what they drank and ate was anyone's guess; it must have been mighty crowded though, but while the crackers were being pulled, I was still not enjoying that powered substitute that was not getting any better.

As we moved into the New Year everyone was feeling rather bloated, they had probably gorged themselves through a mountain of food and drink in the past seven days, the greedy buggers.

Eat, drink and sleep, but it was traditional, the people of this city must have been saving up all year for this week of over indulgence.

All the local shops ran Christmas clubs. For a few shillings a week the ladies, which included my mother and gran, would become eager participants of this saving scheme/pastime.

With the early months of 1956 behind me, I was looking forward to enjoying the sunshine for the very first time.

But what was it with these local and national customs, the kids had just about got over devouring about a million selection boxes at Christmas, now they were repeating the feat with bloody Easter eggs.

We would head for Longley Park and the infamous open air swimming pool and spend time watching the kids daring one another to make the icy plunge!

Even though it was the summer of 1956 and the sun was beating down, it was rumoured that the park keeper had to remove the ice every morning because the water was so cold!

The majestic Forum picture house had kids lined up outside every Saturday morning, and they didn't half make a racket while waiting for the cinema manager to open the doors.

They would see the latest offering which had been shipped over the Atlantic from a place called America.

These included great icons of the time like Roy Rogers, Flash Gordon and Tarzan.

Further down Herries Road was the imposing Five Arches Bridge.

It looked monumental in all its glory and would proudly support the passing trains whether they carried coal destined for the local power stations or passengers who would embark at the nearby Wadsley Bridge Station, when they'd travelled from wherever to visit nearby Hillsborough the home of Sheffield Wednesday Football Club.

Here you can see me relaxing in Hillsborough Park, (I think that is my father in the prone position, did he not like having his photograph taken?)

You also see that I'm wearing a bib again when posing for the cameras, would it have been too much trouble to have removed it before taking this photograph.

It was now time to blow the flame out on my very first candle and knowing full well that in a month's time, old Father Christmas would be giving number 20 Musgrave Road my second visit.

Last time around I'd know idea what the fuss was all about but would this time be any different.

The town would be dressed up with festive lights, and a great big Christmas tree would sit proudly at the top of Fargate, one thing I can say was that I was always taken to town to see the Christmas lights.

While they were preparing for this festive period, presents would have been purchased and the house would have been decorated in all the finery that was associated with the period, and standing in all its glory would be the family Christmas tree, every household had one and ours was topped off with a silver fairy.

On the eve of Christmas I was still sharing a bedroom with my parents, did all the kids of Sheffield do this?

Or was it only me who had grabbed the short straw with open arms!

We awoke to find that Father Christmas had called on the family, so the kids of the household must have behaved themselves. Don't think I did much ripping and tearing of my presents, but Fred and Mick were enjoying themselves.

The traditional dinner would have been lovingly prepared by my Grandma, and probably the grownups of the family may have visited the local public house before dinner was served.

They were stuffing themselves with that joint of meat because a bloody turkey was certainly off the menu in our household. Vegetables were in an abundance and I was at last able to join in with this joyful event.

So now all the family enjoyed the festive spirit; it had not passed me by this time, I must have had something to open, but what it was, will remain a mystery forever.

You see I have got no photographic evidence that dear old Santa ever sat me on his knee.

We had now passed through 1956 and entered '57, I was still shacked up with my parents and the house was still a bit overcrowded, this must have been hard on them not having a house to call home.

I cannot really imagine what those days were like, returning home from work and not having a minute's peace and quiet.

Here we have my two guardian angels Grandma Florence and Auntie Lillian; they were always by my side.

But I was too young to understand and grasp the situation, mind you I was hardly ever in, my two elderly companions were always around once they'd seen to their own families.

Here I am enjoying the lovely weather on another adventure with them, even though their children had moved on in years, these two were always playing the role of my surrogate mothers and boy did I thrive in their company.

We loved it when the weather turned for the better and could enjoy the delights of what this city could offer!

Sometimes we'd head in the other direction from Hillsborough and make the steep descent down Cookswood Road and pass through Burngreave and the Wicker before reaching our final destination.

The old Sheaf Market, or as it was known locally the Rag and Tag Market, at the bottom of Dixon Lane.

The Lane had market stalls that ran the length of it, the stallholders mainly sold fruit and vegetables, but these hardy souls had no cover to shelter from the elements when the weather turned for the worse.

Now the Sheaf was a lively old place with its rows upon rows of market stalls that were made of wood and were sheltered by tin roofs, you could purchase anything there and boy was it thronged with people.

Every couple of weeks I'd be dropped into the big scales that sat proudly at the markets entrance, just to see how my weight was progressing.

They were very popular with the good folk of this city, and you'd always have to queue and wait your turn.

Also visited was the Norfolk Market Hall, this had survived the wartime bombing, and was such another lively place, but this time all the stalls that were bristling with goods, were under cover, unlike the poor souls who worked out in all weathers at the nearby Sheaf.

Again people were enjoying the delights of the Norfolk Arms and its famous Jubilee Stout, but not us; we were making the return journey home, but this time we'd take that lovely blue and cream bus. The driver would be upfront in his cab while the conductor or conductress would pirouette around the pole at the back while dispensing tickets and ringing the bell.

Sheffield was still bearing the scars of war, big gaps occurred where once proud buildings stood

Things were great in my own little world, everyone was looking out for me and now I was well and truly on the way to enjoying birthday number two.

Sheffield Victoria Station transported you in no time to the Lancashire coast, Blackpool was a favourite destination for those Sheffielders who had a free weekend.

I'd already enjoyed one trip to the seaside and was pictured on some rocks looking rather dashing!

Mind you that bloody bib was making another guest appearance for everyone to see; what was it with my guardians, whoever was responsible was an idle bugger, it could have been removed in a few seconds.

It was on that trip to Blackpool that I enjoyed my first ever ride on a donkey, that great British seaside tradition.

These family outings were rare, probably once a year you'd get the chance to put your feet in the sea and play in the sand.

I had not yet grasped the art of cricket, something that lives with me to this day, but it was a great piece of equipment for digging in the sand, please take note that the bloody bib is still hanging around my neck, when I finally lost that piece of material is anyone's guess, but for the time being, it was permanently fastened to me!
But once that was over it was back to reality and the house we called home on our sprawling council estate of Shirecliffe.

Musgrave Road backed onto the Meadows, which gave a great view of the valley that stretched to Owlerton Stadium.

Shirecliffe was a typical housing estate of the time, with Herries Road acting as a boundary from the nearby Longley and Southey estates; we also had the picturesque Meadows behind us.

Most relatives lived within walking distance and getting a house on any of the cities estates must have been increasingly difficult if you wanted to stay local.

You had everything you wanted on your doorstep, and most were within easy reach; local schools being Shirecliffe Nursery, Junior and Infants plus the Secondary for the bigger kids, shops that lined Herries Road, the public houses which included the Five Arches and Devonshire.

Two cinemas, the Forum and Essoldo, and for the more recreational activities you had the parks at Longley which boasted the swimming pool and Hillsborough; there was also one at Firth Park that boasted a nice paddling pool and a lake where the kids could sail their toy boats.

I was still sharing the same room as my parents, that would never happen today, I mean brothers and sisters are certainly not allowed to share in this day and age, so sharing with your parents would never be permitted.

Being housed with so many people meant that there was always somebody in or around the house, and it was a lively old place.

Neighbours were always popping in for a cuppa and a chat, and the atmosphere would ring out with laughter.

But we were still mighty overcrowded in the family home and this created tension amongst the family.

And even though my parents tried their hardest to come to terms with the situation, the bubble was about to burst with an almighty bang!

Things were not so great for my mother and father, endless rows and slanging matches it could not have been easy living like they did;

Things came to ahead after I'd enjoyed my birthday and welcomed in 1958.

Arabian Knight of Neepsend

My father walked out and returned to his mothers in nearby Neepsend, I could not believe that my father had done one, and abandoned yours truly, bloody hell I'd only just blown the candles out on my second birthday cake, (if I'd actually had one!) but at least I'd enjoyed another family Christmas.

What was I going to do? One thing was for certain it was highly unlikely that I would pack my bags and make my own way in this fair city.

George Henry and Florence Emily welcomed him back with open arms, because they never felt Jean was good enough for their only child.

Even though my parents were not the greatest when it came to child welfare, I was fortunate enough to have two Florence Nightingales fighting my corner, whether it was up on the Shirecliffe or down across those Meadows in Neepsend.

Florence Emily Greenwood was born in 1889 and was married to William Brayshaw in the parish of Owlerton in 1912; they had a daughter called Edith.

William answered the call to arms and enlisted to fight for King and Country when war was declared in 1914.

Sad news was delivered to the Brayshaw household, when Florence was told that her husband had been killed in action while fighting in France.

William had given the ultimate sacrifice anyone can ever bequeath on his Country, when he gave up his life fighting for freedom in a foreign land.

Florence had to quickly come to terms with the fact that at the age of 27 she was now a war widow with a daughter to look after.

In 1921 she met a George Henry Cronshaw, a bachelor from Runcorn in Lancashire; he had made the journey over from the red to the white rose county seeking employment, and had settled in the Owlerton district.

George Henry had survived the Great War, but things were hard when he returned, so he made the choice to seek employment in Sheffield.

One minute he was living in a tiny bedsit, then the next he was on the verge of getting married for the very first time. They married the very same year, Edith was now aged nine and George had got himself a ready-made family.

George Henry loved nothing better than enjoying a day at the races most weekends, after he'd finished his job as a wood turner.

Mind you it must have been a 100/1 outsider that after 10 years of marriage to find out he was going to be a father at the age of 50.

James Cronshaw was born on the 31st of March 1931 at the family home at number 112 Hoyland Road, and for most of his childhood it was his step sister Edith who would look after him while his parents continued their love of the sport of kings.

His elder sibling was some 19 years his senior and was a ready-made babysitter, by the time my father was enjoying his school years at Neepsend School, Edith had married a William Harrison and they too joined George Henry and Florence at such places as Doncaster and Pontefract races while dear old father fended for himself back in Sheffield 6.

Father had many friends around the neighbourhood and when not at school, they would get up to mischief any which way they could.

The nearby power station had buckets that deposited the burning embers onto what was known locally as "the burning tip", the kids would ride the returning buckets once they had deposited their load.

The train would slowly climb the hill that led to the power station, and again they would enjoy another free ride, it was like their very own personal Alton Towers.

The local railway workers would have cabins adjacent to the railway, kids would raid them after they had clocked off for the day.

Tizer and Jusoda were a plenty, every kid had a little sip, and the workers would not miss a small drop.

Father remembers one time when the Tizer tasted funny, you see the workers had realised that someone was pinching their daily drink, so they had deposited a good ration of urine into the bottle, this had the little local urchins spluttering all over the inside of the cabin.

They also had these small explosive devices that they would position on to the track to warn them of oncoming trains, when the train ran over them they would explode and give off a warning signal.

The kids would place the charges on to a steel billet, while another billet would be held up by a piece of wood which had string attached, when the kids were ready they'd yank the wood away, thus resulting in the billets making contact with the charge, and BANG!

Those famous Neepsend gas tanks that withstood all that old Adolf Hitler could throw at them, the area had its fair share of bombs dropped on it, and even dropping incendiary bombs did not deter the hardy souls of the neighbourhood.

They just climbed to the top of the tanks, put two fingers up to the Nazi bombers, and booted the burning embers to the streets below.

They had saved the day, and stopped the local school from being blown to kingdom come, to the disappointment of the young street urchins who would have fancied having a six year holiday from the rigorous educational system.

When the war was over the streets were once again restored to their former glory, and all the bomb damage was neatly tidied up.

The kids could now play in the knowledge that the dirty old Germans were not ever again going to litter the area with their filthy bombs.

It was only when playtime was over did father return to an empty house; during the week everyone was at work and come the weekend they would head for the pub or the races, and father would be left to fend for himself.

Hillfoot Council School, that was situated just off Hoyland Road, was not far to travel to school for my father from the age of five.

He was not that keen on the education system and even though he attended regularly, he did not enjoy his schooling.

He tried his best to learn what was on the agenda, but he just did not have a very good temperament for taking it all in, there were too many distractions.

He was always getting into trouble, one such occasion he had a run in with a local girl and in a fit of temper retorted to her having a bit of a scabby face.

The following day he was summoned to the Headmasters office to find the girl and her irate mother stood there, he received three strokes of the cane on each hand, just for name calling.

Schooling was very strict and any form of misbehaviour was met with brute force, imagine spending nine years in that environment, one step out of line and it was six of the Headmasters best to the hand or the arse.

He was hit with all kinds of objects including that flying piece of wood that they dusted the chalk off the blackboard with.

He finally left school at the age of fourteen and started his working life straight away; he was now contributing to the family's weekly meagre budget.

His first job was at a company called Arron Hildick that made all things wood, it was his father George Henry being a wood turner himself that got him the start in the first place.

He was only the yard lad, fetching and carrying the timber for the craftsmen, tidying up after them and being a right old dogsbody.

Next stop for him was Lewis Harvey, a fishmonger in the Sheffield Fish market near Dixon Lane; again he was only a couple of years in this job before at the age of 18 he needed to do his National Service.

Before he enlisted he enjoyed a great social life and liked nothing finer than turning out for the nearby Neepsend Social Club, and he was also a keen supporter of Sheffield Wednesday Football Club.

He first watched the Owls as a six year old in 1937 but his football watching days were eventually curtailed thanks to those Germans who were seeking world domination.

He joined the Kings Own Yorkshire Light Infantry and was proud to be called Private Cronshaw 22154967; his number that he remembers to this day.

Father left his parental home and headed for his training, loads and loads of square bashing was to follow before he proudly boarded the HMS Lancashire to make the four week crossing to Malaya.

He was sent to Malaya because the plantation owners were coming under attack from the Communist Guerrillas, and the British Government decided to send in our troops.

Even though he tried his hardest to be a model soldier, he was not really cut out for life in the Army and finished up in the glasshouse for discharging his rifle while cleaning it, he'd not checked if the gun was empty and luckily for his platoon patrol it was only a cup that finished up being shot!

When he returned to barracks he was placed on guard duty and on one such patrol he landed himself in further bother when he fell, head first, into an inspection pit.

He was transferred to a military hospital to recuperate.

While laid up his replacement joined his ten man patrol, and on one such advance into the jungle the men came under enemy fire which resulted in seven soldiers being killed and the other three were wounded.

This affected my father badly and from that day he could not wait to finish his military service. He was eventually de-mobbed in 1952 and returned home to Sheffield.

My father is the one in the centre, and he looks a picture of health after soaking up all that Tropical sunshine.

After all that sun it was back to the murky streets of Sheffield and returned to work in our prestigious steel industry.

It was at Daniel Doncasters on Penistone Road that he worked to forget about his brief but eventful stint in the army, he made some great friends while serving in the forces. William Jessops and then Hatfields had my father clocking on, in the following few years, it was while working at Hatfields he met his close friends Derek and Arthur.

This is James enjoying a well-earned pint in the Farfield public house; he had done his National Service, and was now back in Civvy Street, he was young free and single.

This was his local; a relaxing place on your

doorstep that was unlike today, filled to the rafters most evenings, no fancy plastic public houses back then, certainly no kids running about the place, and dining was certainly off the menu.

Look at those historical pint pots that must have weighed a ton, the man must have been enjoying his final years of freedom before he finally followed in that great tradition of walking down the aisle and getting hitched to the opposite sex.

He liked socialising in the local pubs and clubs and was fond of the Black Swan or Mucky Duck as it was known locally, it was on one of these outings that he met my mother Jean and after a brief courtship they got married in 1954.

Here you see my father and his mate Arthur, chatting up some lady, these boys were dressed in the finest gear that they had purchased from good old Barney Goodman, Sheffield's finest tailor of his time; you would have to save for weeks to afford one of his suits, once fully kitted out you were ready for the town or fanny brown as it was commonly known.

The Black Swan was situated on Angel Street, and had a great big black swan over its entrance; most weekends it was the singers or groups that kept you entertained.

The Sheffield folk would say that there was a good turn on at the Mucky Duck this Saturday who it was was anyone's guess.

It also ran a weekly talent show where anyone who fancied it could get up and sing their hearts out.

The pub belonged to Samuel Smiths and it sold the finest Tadcaster Ales, mind you whenever we got the chance to taste that mucky looking brew it tasted awful; give us Tizer any day of the week.

Back in Neepsend my father would finish work on a Friday, rush home to meet my mother on the dirt track that ran from Hoyland Road across the Meadows and finish up in Longley Avenue West.

They would rendezvous about half way and I would be exchanged and taken back with my father to spend the weekend with him.

As soon as I reached the front door Gran would strip me and have me stand in the pot sink that overlooked our back garden and outside privy.

There I could see magical smoke coming from the hole in the door, cascading like some spirit from a genies lamp, magical and mystique like a scene from the Arabian nights.

Then the sound of the flush would put paid to my youthful imagination, with the appearance of George Henry clutching the racing paper and puffing on his pipe.

I would then be dried in loving and caring arms and then adorned with a new set of clothes she had purchased, I would be fed and watered and then placed in a massive armchair.

Across from me sat my Granddad and while he was billowing out enough smoke to fill

the room, he always directed it towards the chimney.

He would sit for hours cutting old newspapers into squares and with the help of an old knitting needle he would carefully thread a piece of string through the holes, when he'd got a plentiful supply for the outside loo he'd tie the string together and place it on the nail behind the door.

George Henry at present had plenty of time on his hands because he was currently unemployed, you see he was working at Samuel Osborne's and had a run in with this foreman, he seemed to be on my Granddads back every minute of every day, even though he was pulling his weight and had no complaints off his fellow colleagues, this chap would not leave him alone.

One day George Henry just snapped and flattened the bullying foreman, he gave him a right old leathering to the delights of his workmates but the management sided with the foreman and Granddad was instantly dismissed.

I would have loved to have witnessed that incident, I watched as those same hands lovingly cut those pieces of paper, and threaded them through that string, I used to love sitting on his knee, he had an habit of spitting on the roaring fire, once I copied him and got a right clip round the ear off my Grandma and so did George Henry.

My gran Florence Emily the other nightingale that was constantly fighting my corner,

would always welcome me with open arms when I put my tiny feet over her neatly donkey stoned front step.

Her daughter Edith only lived a few doors away at number 100 Hoyland Road, and I would often witness mother and daughter donkey stoning their steps in unison.

My Gran was probably the first one that introduced me to the art of mathematics, because she would place me in the darkened cellar and instruct me to count the bags of coal that the merchant deposited through the cellar grate, she did not trust him and was constantly harping on that he was leaving her a bag short when he made his delivery, I always brought a smile to her face when I uttered the words, number six.

Once that job was done I would be ceremonially dumped into the pot sink again that overlooked the throne room, or outside toilet where the smoke was still billowing out for all to see.

While there I would visit friends and neighbours and make the short trip to the park and then on our return would be treated to some sweets from Mrs Balm's shop that stood on Neepsend Road; the bell would ring as you entered the premises, and I would gaze at rows upon rows of sweets in glass jars, my father would point and the lady would tip them into the scales, before emptying them into a paper bag.

I would then be passed the contents with the words "Now don't you eat them all at once, save some for later" left ringing in my ears!

My excursion would last until Sunday afternoon, then I would be handed back to my mother who would whisk me away from my father without a word being spoken, I would wave but his back would be turned as he trudged back towards home.

Once back at Musgrave Road I would again be stripped of my new attire, which would be thrown towards the darkest corner of the room, again it was bath time but instead of the pot sink these houses had a bath upstairs.

My parents were at this time not a guiding light for this two year old, but I did have in my favour both my Grandma's.

I was still sleeping in my mother's room, and during the day it was my guardian angels Flo and Lily who cared for my every need, while my mother went to work.

This lasted another six months before mother and father decided to re-unite the family and James returned to Shirecliffe.

Things were fine and everyone was getting on like a house on fire, this upset my Neepsend side of the family slightly but they realised it was for the best.

Things Can Only Get Better

The year was now 1958 and Sheffield was well and truly over the war years and the city was steadily getting back to its former glory.

The glorious trams were still running but the buses were just about starting to take control, mind you the better off people, (which we were not one of them,) owned their own motor transport in the shape of a car, while the fool hardy tried to negotiate the track laden streets on their bicycles!

I was now getting out and about on my own, and would spend hours in my proper back garden on the Shirecliffe, while over at Neepsend it was just a back yard but it was safe. I was now three years of age and would gaze over the Meadows and see Owlerton Stadium in the distance, this place hosted greyhound and speedway racing, the latter would fill the air with the roar of motorbike engines waiting to be unleashed onto the circular track, many a night we would sit and listen to the noise that was drifting across the valley.

Here I am pictured with my faithful companion enjoying the delights of my own space, that dog went everywhere with me and it never left my side.

I was kind of oblivious to what was happening around me, for god sake I was a kid doing what kids did, that was eat, drink and play.

While our household was experiencing this turbulent period, with mother and father at loggerheads, the local catholic priest would visit to lend a helping hand.

Or was he just taking a keen interest in this child who was being shunted from one house to another?

Shirecliffe was a bustling estate and there always seemed to be something going on, you see there was everything you wanted on your doorstep.

After enjoying myself all day with the family, my joy turned to tears when I realised mother had gone and done one this time, now she had fled the family home and had it on her toes.

Mind you she only lasted a few weeks before she asked to come back, father thought that it would be for the best, after he'd previously gone AWOL as well.

The reconciliation seemed to have done the trick, because during the summer of 1959 we were gearing ourselves up to enjoy our first ever family holiday, when at long last Grandma waved us goodbye as we headed towards Skegness and the resort of Ingoldmells.

We travelled by train to spend a whole week in some caravan by the seaside, and boy was I going to enjoy myself, my father even played cricket with me on the beach, no more shouting matches, I'd even got to enjoy my very own bedroom!

Why could we not take this caravan back to Sheffield and place it in our back garden? For the very first time in my short life, harmony had been the key word, but would it last once we had returned home to join the rest of the family?

I'd loved it at the seaside and enjoyed being centre of attention; all this fresh sea air must have had a calming effect on my parents because not a harsh word was spoken between them.

I was nearing my introduction to the education system and I was still sleeping in the same room as my parents.

How trendy am I looking in this picture, I may not have got the greatest parents in the world, but they certainly knew how to dress and groom me.

My father would take me to the barbers on Blonk Street after we had manoeuvred our way along the bustling Wicker, I would be placed on a box that sat on that Barber's chair, and well I was only a little lad, after this was done we would visit the market to buy great delights like Finny Haddock, Tripe or Chickling and Bag, and boy did that place stink.

It was a kind of Saturday morning ritual of all the folk of Sheffield to descend on the place, and purchase the foulest looking dishes money could buy.

I settled for a bag of sweets or a nice ice cream, they must have tasted a million times better than that Tripe that everyone was fighting over.

When we returned from that holiday the family upped sticks and moved across the Meadows to share the other family home in Neepsend, they were hoping that the change of scenery and living arrangements would kick start their marriage, but it was all in vain, because the ladies of the house could just not get on.

They were always slagging one another and the battles were endless.

Now it was mother's turn to run for the hills; she slammed that door for the final time and sprinted back to Musgrave Road.

I was now, for the time being at least, in the loving hands of Florence Emily. My guardians better get my life sorted soon because I was gearing myself up to start on the long road of the educational system.

But would I be following in my father's footsteps and enrolling at the school in Neepsend?

Father made the decision for me. We packed our bags, waved goodbye to Hoyland Road and returned to Musgrave Road, dragged from pillar to post sprang to mind, but I was only a kid and did not let the situation affect me, I was too busy doing things that four year olds do.

It was September 1959, and the call had come, Shirecliffe Nursery School had given me a 12 month contract and the day was getting for ever closer, but what would it be like? Would I enjoy it and what would the other kids be like?

I was now old enough to join in the early morning get together which involved having lovely brown toast and piping hot tea. As soon as I'd finished I was out of the door with my mother dragging me down Longley Avenue West.

I'd never been out of the house this early, and I could see kids being dragged in the distance towards this white washed outhouse that looked no bigger than George Henry's privy in Neepsend.

I was ushered through very large gates and into the white washed brick building, and made to sit on the tiniest most uncomfortable chair I'd ever encountered; sat next to me was this snotty nosed kid who'd never seen a slab of carbolic!

My mother was talking to this woman one minute, then a quick wave and she was off out of the door, bloody hell I thought had I been left again!

Where on earth was I, some kind of workhouse for abandoned children?

I expected the priest coming through the door any minute to play take your pick.

Well if he did, old snot box would be ok.

Tears started to dwell in my eyes and my lips started to quiver, and that was it, I erupted like an emotional volcano and boy did I blow!

I was in full flow when the woman homed in on me and put a plastic apron around my neck, I know I was having a good crying session but give over lady, I don't think I'm going to get wet through.

Once the apron was securely fastened I was steered towards a very large plastic sink that was full of water and given a plastic beaker, there were four other kids around me and we all started playing happily with our mugs.

I was dipping mine in and pouring it into different sized vessels that adorned the sink and I was enjoying myself. Over the other side of the room more kids were doing the same but instead of water they'd got sand, they were filling little shells and making miniature sandcastles, while over in the other direction kids were slapping paint onto paper and it was going everywhere!

My tears had completely dried and I loved every minute of it, I'd forgotten all about my mother who had left me here.

I was now in full swing when this bell went; the lady hurriedly took all the water, sand and paint off everybody.

Off came the protective aprons and we were made to sit around our tables again, and I was not liking this and not sure what was going to happen next?

Suddenly the door opened and in walked this man carrying two crates, the lady started to hand out tiny bottles of milk and straws, now this was getting better, not only did they let you play they gave you milk as well, but what would they want in return I thought to myself?

Once the milk had been consumed the lady took out a very large book and started to read us a story, blimey another first in my life someone reading to me, mind you come to think of it I don't think I had any books!

I was really liking my new home even though sniffles at the side of me was doing my head in, this was great and I thought this was the life, when that bell went again and I thought what more milk?

My hopes were dashed when mother reappeared along with other females all making a beeline for the different array of kids on view, even snot box was reunited with his mother, and off we all went.

My mother asked me how my first day was at school.

I excitedly told her about the water, sand, paint and we got to drink milk!

Gran had got my dinner ready, the day was getting better and now I was on top of the world. On arriving home it was nice to sit on a comfortable chair while I told Gran about my day at school, she said they'll be plenty of time for chat but in the meantime finish your dinner you've got to be back at school in half an hour.

I've got to go back?

Now that was a shock to the system!

Yeah I'd enjoyed myself but I thought I'd rather stay here and play with my toy soldiers. But back I had to go; this was my first introduction to our country's fine educational establishment.

Even old snotty had made another session but surely his mother knew that he had green coloured dew drops hanging from his nose end.

I let this day pass but if he sat next to me tomorrow then his dew drops would turn crimson!

The bell went again mid-afternoon and we enjoyed a drink of water and another story, and before I knew it there was another ringing of the bell and I was off out into my mother's arms, I'd really enjoyed myself and looked forward to what tomorrow had in store.

I managed to cop for a treat on the way home - my favourite chocolate bar called Five Boys. It pictured some kid whose face changed from sad to happy in five easy stages, a bit like me considering my circumstances; mind you I was more happy than sad thankfully.

None more so when mum took the time to take me out, we would head for Attercliffe and the imposing department store called Banners. It was an Aladdin's Cave for small boys, there must have been a whole floor dedicated to toys.

I would gaze and drool over the rows and rows of toy soldiers, but I was only allowed two per visit. Would it be a cowboy or an Indian, or would it be a soldier from the war? It would take me bloody ages to choose, one day though when I got home and emptied my pockets of them into my biscuit tin, I must have had a whole bloody platoon in there.

It was the my first introduction into the 'buy one get one free' culture, or was it just plain old shoplifting? I was far too young to understand that what I was doing was wrong, but my tin was full to bursting.

I was now four years of age and we were just about to embark on the Swinging Sixties. The start of the new decade seemed to have a calming influence on my parents and things were progressing nicely.

William Jnr had just got married and for a moment I thought he'd be bringing his new bride home, but our Bill was not daft; he had sorted out his own sleeping arrangements when he purchased his own house in Grenoside.

As we progressed through the year, I noticed that my mother had really clapped on the weight and looked rather chubby, I thought I'd better keep this to myself, don't want to go and upset her now do I?

One morning, just before I was getting ready for school, my mother let out an almighty scream and she was off out of the door clutching a case. Bloody hell I thought, am I being left again?

But never mind that, I was too busy enjoying the toast that Gran had prepared for me. Why had she gone?

What had I done?

At least father was at work so he was oblivious to my predicament, wasn't I thankful that I'd got good old Grandma fighting my corner.

Even when father returned he demolished his tea and he was off out without a word being spoken, I'd really drawn the short straw with these two for parents, I was in tears but nobody seemed to be interested apart from him with the black frock and the cross around his neck, he just kept tapping me on my head.

Next day they both returned, but my mother's weight had disappeared, had she been to some health camp that reduced your size overnight?

All the neighbours were congregating outside the house and I saw them looking at the bundle my father was carrying.

Nice one I thought, a new toy for yours truly. Everyone was prodding and poking it, yes the great mystery had been solved, my baby brother had been born on the 16th of April 1960 and now just after we'd got shut of young William we get another bloody lodger. I climbed the stairs to get out of the way of all this fuss. The baby was named Mark, bloody Mark what kind of name was that? Had the old girl got a soft spot for all things

Italian? I can just see it now in another year's time, out pops little baby Caesar!

This time though it's me not the two boys who had to share with the new arrival, not only have I got my parents to put up with but the racket that a new born baby brings, it was not good! Would my schooling suffer?

I'd enjoyed my first taste the educational system, and now it was time to move up to the infants, no more playing in the water and sand, this was serious stuff! Every morning my hair would be neatly combed and my mother would work over-time with the flannel! I had a nice white shirt, knitted jumper and a pair of fashionable trousers, boy I looked smart! After my birthday I would always wear a poppy with much pride, as I still do to this day.

We had to sit two to a desk, and would be given an exercise book, pencil and rubber where we would learn to spell and do sums. Book reading was also on the curriculum.

It was in infant school that I was introduced to Christopher Bartholomew (2313), Wesley Haywood (2325) and Glen Fearn (2323) (my very first friends in the outside world).

Everyone child was issued with a number at the start of their schooling, mine just happened to be 2314; we all set out on this educational trail on the 6th of September 1960.

We would have to wait until the 9TH of January 1961 to be introduced to John Gallagher (2350) thus completing our gang of five line up.

I was now nearing my fifth birthday and loved my schooling, probably it was a respite from family life and this time you could pick and choose who you wanted to spend time with.

Our kid was nearly six months old and he'd got the blondest hair you'd ever seen, he looked like a girl; mind you it came in handy at Whitsuntide!

Whitsuntide was that good old Christian festival, it rivalled Christmas, Good Friday, Easter Day and Ascension Day.

The festivities would start on the Saturday when everyone would go for a stroll in the park, it was a fun day for all the family. On the Sunday though it really got serious, tradition had it, that all the children would be kitted out in brand new clothing, and we were no exception.

On Whitsuntide Sunday you would be thrown in the bath, receive an almighty scrubbing including your ears and then made to put on your new clothes and shoes.

First up you'd be paraded round the near neighbours and in return for you walking the local catwalk, they'd bung you some coins of the realm, our neighbours were very generous especially the elderly because they could remember the days when their children would be dressed to kill.

Next up it would be Auntie Lillian and Uncle Frank, even though they were not related, I treated them like family members, Frank was always sound for a couple of shilling.

Then it would be my mother's relatives, the Marriott's on the Southey. I'd been dragged from here to there all day, and these new clothes and shoes were killing me, before finally we would walk down Halifax Road and Penistone Road before arriving totally knackered in Neepsend. I would not even be allowed out to play and had sit on the hardest chair that was stuck in the corner - at least our Mark had a comfy pram to nod off in.

On Whit Monday it was back to the park to listen to the bands playing their array of musical instruments, everyone seemed to be in a very good mood, mind you the kids looked bored to tears and they could not wait for the racket to finish.

I was now getting totally pissed off with this Whit malarkey, I know we had received some nice new clothes and had got a tin full of pennies, three penny bits, sixpences and a couple of shillings.

Again we were out of the house, but this time our clothes were of the old playful variety, thank god for that, I was at last getting the chance to play.

We walked down Longley Avenue West in the direction of the Five Arches public house, there were crowds everywhere, they were lined the length of Herries Road, both sides of the road was bustling with people.

We took up our position in the Arches car park, all the family was in attendance, including Uncle Frank and Auntie Lily, it turned out that we were waiting for that Whit Tuesday Sheffield Tradition, the Star Walk, it had first taken place on the 6th of June 1922, the entrants had to stump up a shilling to take part back then, over the years the route had been changed several times, but now in the Sixties once they had left the Star Building in High Street at 10am prompt, it made its way towards Hillsborough before passing the football ground via Leppings Lane, again it climbed Halifax Road until it reached the Norfolk Arms in Grenoside, down through Whitley before reaching Ecclesfield, the walkers then climbed again and headed for the Pheasant at Sheffield Lane Top.

I must have walked as far the previous Sunday and even though I was only 5 years of age, I'm sure I'd have given them a run for their money.

The intrepid contestants had now made their way onto Herries Road opposite the Devonshire, we could hear the crowds in the distance cheering on the leaders, now it was our turn and I was sat on my father's shoulders to get a bird's eye view, I cheered along with everyone, this was more like it , this is what I called a fun day out. We cheered every single walker from the first to the last, the weather was great for us but as the stragglers disappeared out of view, I thought most of them would be knackered. I was thinking of carting my brother out of his pram, so I could give these that were finding it difficult a helping hand.

We finished off such a terrific day with a nice bag of crisps and a bottle of pop; I had really enjoyed myself watching that great local tradition, the Sheffield Star Walk.

Our family seemed to have settled down now and no more slanging matches, well not when we were in earshot; mind you Frederick and Michael were still at home, so we were still a bit overcrowded.

We'd progressed nicely as a family and I was enjoying school evermore and was getting more freedom to spend time with my friends, even though we were not allowed to move

off our street.

I would spend hours kicking a ball around on the back garden, or when we visited my Gran at Neepsend a tennis ball would be provided so I could play in relative safety in Hoyland Road. Our Mark following in my footsteps and enjoying a ride on a donkey, I am obscured in this photo, which is a blessing because I'd had my bloody head shaved.

Mind you the dummy and bloody bib had been passed on, and for once it was not dangling around my neck, I was not quite sure if we had returned to Ingoldmells, but my money was on that this was good old Blackpool beach, the reason being that you can see the sea, so it certainly wasn't Cleethorpes.

My Florence Nightingale

Once again I was out the door early with my mother but this time instead of heading for school we were on the bus, just like that one pictured above, and off in the direction of town. I could not understand why I was not going to school, we were not on holiday, I was not sick so the hospital was out of the question.

Mother hardly said a word as we made our way into town, once we'd alighted it was onto another bus and off we went again.

I was now in unfamiliar territory and had no idea where I was heading; I don't think I'd ever been on two separate buses in my life before!

We passed the policeman who was always orchestrating the traffic and headed to the top of Fargate, but now the Christmas tree had disappeared.

I was gazing out of the window and noticed that other childhood institution that went by the name of Redgates that place outshone Banners because it was a kiddie's paradise.

I could have lived in that place with its magic train sets, that were securely tucked away behind sheets of glass, no chance of the little urchins having that lot away.

Again we were off and trudging the streets and these houses headed for the sky, how tall were they, I

looked up and could not see the top.

We stopped at this stairwell and started to climb and climb, step upon step we took and came to a sudden stop outside this brightly painted front door with the number 13 adorning it, (unlucky for some I thought,) looking down through the concrete pillars that reminded me of my very first abode in the hospital.

Mother knocked on the door and then this giant opened it and gave her a kiss, now this was not an auntie or uncle kiss, bloody hell I thought he could do with a good wash, he was as black as the ace of spades!

Just like that bloke who brought that stuff we threw on the fire and when you touched that it came off on your hands leaving a black stain on your fingers, I thought if mother doesn't stop it she'll be covered in it. In we went and I was ceremonially dumped on the kitchen floor and told "be a good boy and play with your car".

I was now alone and it felt like ages before they reappeared with mother looking rather flustered and the coal man looked out of breath as well.

This scenario was repeated again and again and I hated it, I hated the bus journey, the walk to the flats, the stairs that we had to climb and most of all I hated the coalman he scared me no end.

It was only me who had to encounter this charade because our Mark was left with Grandma.

One day when mother was out and we were in the care of Grandma Flo, I let rip and blurted out that I hated our trip across town to see the mucky looking man who could do with a good scrub with a giant slab of carbolic soap and would she please have a word with my mother, Gran nearly exploded and used words I'd never heard in my life, she was like a volcano and she'd lost it big time.

Boy was she angry and off she shot upstairs, top of the wardrobe was a suitcase and she lifted it down and proceeded to fill it with my mother's clothes, our Mark was soundly asleep and how he slept through it I'll never know, the case was now full and sat proudly to attention at the top of the stairs.

Gran had tears in her eyes something I'd never witnessed before, to me she was as hard as nails and not one to be messed with, (even granddad steered clear if he'd had one too many from his excursion to the Kings Head,) I kept quiet and thought was it me that had upset her?

Then my mother put her head through the door and that was it, the fully laden suitcase was heading in her direction, how it never took her head off, I'll never know and the two women, mother and daughter went at it like hammer and tongs! Gran was in full control and mother never stood a chance, she was being booted out of the family home and with me and our Mark as the only witnesses and to tell you the truth it was not pleasant viewing, it turned out that the coal man was in fact a man of Caribbean persuasion that mother had met while working on the buses.

It appears that this was going on for ages, and this is where she had been when she disappeared for those few weeks, father had thought it was for the best when she wanted to return to the family home, and for a brief few months we carried on like a normal happy family.

But her feelings for this man must have been stronger than her feelings for her husband, I know marriages break up, when the couples are not compatible, but to leave two children and not ever want contact is something I will never get my head around.

I was now 6 and our Mark had just blown the candles out in the celebration of his first birthday and we were now one parent short for a picnic again, well I was because this was the very first time it had happened to our kid. What was going to happen to us, what would father do?

Would he also abandon us and go back to his mother, he was only 31, how could he bring up two kids on his own? What would Gran do now? We stood on the step that she had just donkey stoned and waved goodbye to mother.

She disappeared into the distance and Gran shut the door, for the time being we were safe and secure but what reaction would our Florence Nightingale get when the others returned to the family home?

Her own kids were now grown up so it would be just my father and my Grandparents on my mother's side who would decide our future. Granddad who just finished his shift on the railway was first home, mind you he'd managed a couple in the boozer before teatime, then my long suffering father returned after he'd just managed a twelve hour shift driving his crane at Hatfield's well that was it what was left of the family were now all together but what would the outcome be?

My Grandmother was no spring chicken, how could she or my father cope? Would we be put into care or would the local priest find us somewhere to live?

Florence took control from the off and even though her own children had all become adults and she'd been a mother to them all for 30 years, she was prepared to start all over again.

Father was adamant she (Jean) was not returning and even though I was not to know it but that day was the very last time I would see my birth mother, but who cared it was apple pie and custard for afters!!

The following weeks saw my Gran grow in stature as she paraded her new kids on the block around the estate, it was now her or the ever reliable side kick Aunt Lily who would take me to school.

My schooling never suffered probably because I was too young to grasp the situation that I found myself in, it also must have been very trying times for my father and although he'd left me once before, this time I knew deep down that he was in this for the duration.

Mind you his work suffered and he was taking more and more time off work which infuriated my Gran and she'd let him know it on numerous occasions.

Father even took me to the pictures on Wordsworth Avenue, I think it was called the Essoldo. Saturday evening and I was going to the pictures, I was wondering what they were serving up for this eager six year old.

One Hundred and One Dalmatians by Walt Disney was breaking all box office records, did we go and see that epic cartoon fantasy? Did we buggers, my father took me to see The Guns of Navarone.

I know it's a classic film, and I can watch it now when it's shown on the television, but there's no wonder I only lasted an hour in the pictures before he dragged me out - I must have had me tucked up in bed before them Germans got blown to pieces.

I don't really know how my father's parents reacted to this very unusual situation but as always they backed their son one hundred per cent, and my visits to Neepsend were still very joyous to say the least.

I loved that little goggle box that sat proudly in the corner at Grans, my all-time favourite programme at the time was Four Feather Falls, but more on that later.

Once school was over for the week, kids would rush home and grab a couple of hours playing to their hearts content, but when that clock moved towards teatime, kids would disappear off the streets and they had not even heard those immortal words, 'get yourselves inside your tea's ready'.

They would sit on that settee, eyes glued to that wooden box, waiting for those words they had been longing for all week, 'its Friday, its five to five and its Crackerjack'.

Screaming kids in the audience would go crazy, the presenters were just as daft, games would be played and the contestants would win prizes for correct answers, but get one wrong and you'd be bunged a cabbage.

The lucky kid who won kept the goodies, while the loser went home with a bloody pencil.

The latest chart offering would be played, and it would always end with a bit of a pantomime, woe betide anyone who would interrupt my Crackerjack moment.

Teatime meals would be eaten stone cold, because those little eyes would be in a trance for nearly an hour, once it was over and the culinary delights were devoured, it was back onto those streets.

Other offerings around the time were the Lone Ranger, Champion the Wonder Horse and William Tell, these would have us replaying their antics on the nearby tip, but the cream was Supercar, Stingray and the impressive Fireball XL5.

How lucky were we to have an abundance of classic kids viewing that kept us indoors for no more than an hour a day, then it would be back out to play once more.

Gran again took control and found it increasingly unhealthy that we were still sharing a room with my father; I mean I had just celebrated my seventh birthday and I was shacked up with dear old dad.

Gran had badgered the council to remedy the situation we found ourselves in. Again she had won the day and in the early part of 1963 we moved to number 23 Musgrave Road. It was just across the road but at long last my dad had his very own rent book and I had my very own family home and my very own bedroom even though I had to share a great big double bed with our kid.

Seven years of age and I spend my first night's sleep in my own room, I must have spent ages in the bath because nobody was hammering on the door like they did at Grans.

Gran would come across every morning while dad was at work and get me ready for school, now it was my turn to enjoy the piping hot tea and rustic toast she served up on a daily basis but this time it was in my own house and in front of my very own fire.

It was not long after we had moved into number 23 that Uncle Fred had got married to Dianne Barnes in 1963 and they moved in with us, I think they struggled to get a house of their own and my Gran thought it would be a good idea to let them share the family home.

Uncle Fred built a great big stone fireplace, and set about making the place look like a home to live in, he carpeted the whole of the upstairs and bought single beds for me and our Mark, this was the first time ever I had managed to acquire a bed of my own in my very own room.

Things were great and for no apparent reason Dianne bought me a new football kit, I think it was one of those you get out of the club book; it was a blue shirt, white shorts and blue socks, a bit like Everton. No more slanging matches and dad who had been retitled by us from the boring father tag, seemed to be happier with judgement day just around the corner, you see he had rebuffed her attempts to come back into our lives and along with my Granddad he was due to visit the courthouse to claim custody of his two boys. We were banking on dear old dad playing a blinder and doing the unthinkable of the time and getting the judge's approval to leave the kids with him, that's the last thing this seven year old needed was to be shipped off to some inner city high rise and live with the dusky coalman.

Dad emerged triumphant, he'd convinced the judge that it was in our best interests to let him have sole custody, mind you she never contested it, so we were best off with her out of our lives, once and for all.

My mates were great company and as we neared the end of our stay in the infants, the thought of moving up to the juniors was quite daunting.

You would be at the mercy of the older kids who were some four years your senior, this never seemed to phase Chris as we made our way home from school every afternoon, we'd heard stories that the first years - which we were soon to become - had their heads pushed down the toilet and the flush pulled; rumour had it that one poor kid had drowned but this was never confirmed!

For the time being we were safe and we'd got the six weeks holidays to look forward to and all the mischief this gang could muster happiness from morning till night.

Now Shirecliffe tip was our happy hunting ground and we'd roam it every spare minute and gasp at what the folk of this fine city were throwing away.

The area was massive; rumour had it that it numbered 300 acres that included the woods of Scraith Wood and the Rawson Wood Spring.

People lived in the prefabricated houses which were built during the war in the wood; we would spend hours in this wood, climbing trees and making dens.

There was also a tunnel that ran under Herries Road and it was a dare to go through it and come out into the fishing pond opposite, you were ok when entering but once in the middle of the tunnel it was pitch black and you had to feel your way along.

Sometimes, when you dared someone to do it for the first time, you would tell them to be careful and take their time, and watch out for the rats!

This gave some of us time to cross the road and enter from the opposite side. We had an old pair of pants that would be soaking wet, and we would wait in the darkness and silence.

As the tunnel virgin inched his way along, just at the right moment we would throw the pants in his direction, nine times out of ten we would get him in the face and he would scream out in panic and turn tail and run, out would come the torch and the pants would be retrieved, and they would sit patiently at the entrance until they were needed again. Further over was the heathland that overlooked the Five Arches bridge and railway line, there was a sheer drop from the top of the heath and many a time you would have a dozen kids inching themselves towards the cliff's edge and peering downwards, we would spend hours just spitting and watching it fall a million feet, we would also throw bricks and try to get them into the empty coal trucks has they were passing, small things occupied our small minds back in the day.

If you headed across the heath, you would come across the Black bridge that led down into Wardsend Cemetery, this place was eerie and unkempt.

It had opened its doors for business back in 1850, and was reported to have 20,000 inhabitants, many of these had come from Hillsborough Barracks, the local workhouse and medical school.

I hated playing in this cemetery and was glad when it was time to move on. Moving along on the banks of the River Don, you would have the bridge that led to the speedway at Owlerton; coming back towards the meadows you now would come across that scary zigzagged shaped passageway that led up to the White bridge, many a time we would use this when we had visited the speedway and after enjoying the delights of the Sheffield Tigers, this was the quickest way home, but you could not see around the corner and it was reported that the local bogey man would be waiting to abduct any unsuspecting child - our hearts were in our mouths every time we did this.

The only other alternative was to go the long way round using Penistone and Herries Road, so we gritted our teeth and chose the hazardous route all the time.

Though we never lost a single child to that bogey man, we were always glad to see the bright street lamps that lit up Penrith Road.

But it was the Shirecliffe tip, or the Sheffield Council landfill site to give it the proper title, that was our favourite play area, and how we spent many a happy time on there.

First job in the summer break was to find an isolated spot and dig for Australia - rumour had it if you were to dig deep enough you'd end up in the land of kangaroos!

Once the hole was about six foot deep (we gave up the dig to Australia!) you could now stand up and not have your head poking out, mission was accomplished.

Now came the tricky part of collecting the timber to cover it up and the lino to waterproof it.

This was our den and many a den would be attacked and smashed, before you could enjoy the fruits of your labour; we never had a problem due to the fact that Chris had three very large big brothers called Winston, Charles and Eric!

In return for them minding our hideaway it was theirs come night fall when they liked to entertain the ladies; we once sneaked in when one of the brothers was wrestling this female and Wes swore he saw her breasts but I was too busy scrabbling to safety after we'd been found out and objects were flying in our direction.

It would take us days to complete the job and our first test would be to see if it was waterproof.

Now with it being the height of summer and the sun beating down from the sky and the prospect of rain non-existent we had only one alternative, we'd draw straws which consisted of four blades of grass that Chris would hold in his hand with the shortest being the loser, we were now ready and I went first and mine must have been a foot long so I was out.

Next stepped Wes and he too drew lucky, it was now up to John to pick and once he'd chosen Chris revealed his.

Poor old Chris had lost so he disappeared from view and shouted that he was ready, he'd armed himself with empty paint pots to catch the drips so we knew which areas needed sorting out, it was now knobs out time and we'd not had a piss all morning and I was bursting, we stood there pissing on the roof while old piss catcher moved the pots to catch the piss.

We were laughing our bollocks off as Chris shouted it's gone down my neck, we never did get it watertight but how we laughed trying to achieve our aim.

The other great feat of construction was getting a fire going without it choking us, this was achieved by digging into the wall of the den and collecting house bricks to create our chimney, nine times out of ten we'd be off target and emerge coughing and spluttering and with a face like my absent mother's fancy man.

I was happy and didn't have a care in the world; I'd rush up to Gran's even though we now had a house of our own, when playtime was over where she'd drag me up into the bath and scrub me white again, how I loved my time spent in the company of my guardian angel.

Mother was now a distant memory and our family was better off without her.

Even though my family life had been a slight turbulent, there was never a dull moment in my social life.

Two of my best mates lived around the corner on Longley Avenue West, Wesley at number 146 while Christopher lived further down the road at 196. These boys I had known from Shirecliffe Infant School and they were always there for me and you could not wish to meet a finer pair of pals anywhere in the world.

On the other side of Herries Road lived Glen Fearn, he had been with me since the days of splashing and painting in school before we moved onto the infants, we would spend every minute of the weekends and school holidays playing on the Meadows, swinging over the River Don on a rope, we even tried to make a raft one time but that sank leaving us all soaking wet!

We'd even venture as far as the Rivelin Valley on our bikes, well I had to borrow one because at present I didn't have one to call my own.

The following day we decided to visit Longley baths, that open aired ice covered swimming pool.

Why we went I never know to this day, the water was freezing, you could only last about five minutes tops, the rest of the time you were rubbing your feet and fingers to get some life back into them.

We had messed about most of the day and now it was time to go home; off we trotted up lovely tree-lined Herries Avenue trying to whip one another with our towels.

Then from nowhere this big dog appeared. It was not kid friendly and it had us scattering in all direction. I just think it wanted to join in our game, but the bastard was striking fear into every jack one of us.

It was a lovely summer's day and to say we were scantily dressed was an understatement. We were trying to climb the trees, and others were jumping through hedges to get away from it.

Chris had the beast hanging off his arse and was hysterical; it lasted about five minutes before this bloke shouted the Hound of the Baskervilles.

It had left a trail of destruction in its wake. Chris had bite marks on his rear end, the kids up the trees were also bleeding from scrambling up them, and those that had leapt through the bushes would be scarred for life.

Chris had to go to the hospital to get stitched up, that bloke with the dog never apologised for his mutt's behaviour, I think Chris's brothers had a few choice words to say to him, and it wouldn't have surprised me if they hadn't bitten the dog themselves.

The teachers were ready and waiting for us in September 1963, our sports master is Vic Spencer who can be seen on the back row to the far right. The holiday was over and we had just about survived another fun packed vacation.

1963 saw me move up to the Junior School, my mates were still there and I again loved my education and the free milk and the lovely school dinners.

But this place was a lot bigger than the infants and the first break of the very first day saw all of the first years bursting for a piss but nobody would venture into the toilets.

Chris broke the deadlock and ventured inside, we heard him kicking and screaming and splashing about, flush after flush then the noise was over, out he emerged his full head of hair soaking wet and his new school shirt ripped to shreds.

He was followed out by a gang of fourth years who were laughing their bollocks off, Chris headed home out of the school gates and missed the rest of the morning session, the teacher was going mental that he had gone AWOL and told us he'd be in front of the headmaster when he returned.

He missed his dinner but returned for the afternoon session and was immediately dragged out of class to face the wrath of the head, he returned shortly with tears in his eyes and a throbbing backside, he'd copped for the slipper for leaving the premises without permission, harsh or what after those bastards had tried to drown him?

The following day, while the rest of us were again pissing our pants, old Chris made for the bogs, this time he fought his corner but was no match for these fourth year tyrants; he was bloody piss wet through again but made no attempt to leave the premises, he sat through the rest of the day in this state and kind of loved the attention.

The bell rang and it was every kid for themselves, get through this first week and we'd survived; the bullies were after anyone they could get their hands on and kids were falling right, left and centre on the playground.

Our lot had made the safety of the school gates, and Chris was beaming like a Cheshire cat, for across the road stood their Charlie, Winston and Eric.

Once Chris had pointed out who his aggressors were the school cheered as the bullies got battered by Longley Avenue West's finest.

I know it was traditional to get your head stuffed down the bog in your first days at school, but ripping the lads shirt when money was tight was a step too far and his elder brothers were always there for their younger sibling.

The fuss soon died down and we were left to enjoy the delights of what school had to offer, I loved it in class but the playground was where it all happened. Sometimes we'd be in school some forty minutes before classes started, coats were down and the tennis ball would be brought out and twenty a side games of football were not uncommon, and games of kick can, finger, thumb and rusty bum were our PSP or PlayStation.

Every day we'd get a bottle of milk; in the summer months it would be like clotted cream and in the winter it would be frozen solid and I loved my job of being the milk monitor because any left overs were yours.

I liked reading, writing, history and art when in the classroom.

I hated maths or sums as we called it and that religious thingy, I mean after the start him upstairs had thrown me what do you expect?

Football and the gym in the winter and cricket, rounders and running in the summer just about put the icing on my educational cake.

During the football season was the only time we'd get the chance to play on the school pitch during our lessons, so on the day you were due to enjoy yourself playing our national game, the kids would be staring out of the windows all morning hoping it did not bleeding rain.

Games as it was called were usually the last lesson before home time and god forbid if it rained, this would mean you skipping and rolling about in the sports hall.

Vic Spencer was our sports master and he was great to have around, a very good football coach who would give all the kids great encouragement.

I loved football and would spend hours cleaning my football boots, this really pissed off the ladies of the household because I always forgot to remove the mud that I had deposited into the sink, I'd get a good clip around the ear; I never did learn my lesson.

I would cake my boots in dubbin before threading my white laces through them; they would sit proudly to attention until the next time we were given the all clear to play on the school fields.

I also had a case ball or Casey as they were fondly known.

This had a lace inserted and the rubber inners would be blown up before being tied with string. In wet weather these balls weighed a ton, and they would nearly take your head off if you managed to connect with it.

I was now eight years of age and quite independent, I would keep myself occupied every minute of every day, dad was always working and paid my Grandmother to keep us fed and clothed, Mark was now three-years-old so he was still in the fulltime care of Flo and Lily and it was now him who they'd take out and about.

Just after I had enjoyed my birthday, it was time to enjoy another great British tradition, it was the 5th of November and the anniversary of old Guy Fawkes trying to blow up the Houses of Parliament.

Now I was not into the political side of his exploits, all I knew was it was yet another money spinner, and when our gang were on the streets in early October we were the best at penny for guying.

During the day though we set about trying to salvage enough timber to light up the whole universe and the big lads would build it as high as the biggest mountain that I thought happened to be in Africa because I read about in a book at school.

The test would come once it was built and the need to stop other kids from outside the area setting it on fire before the big day; everyone would guard it 24/7.

You would try to stay out as long as humanly possible - the big lads sleeping out all night.

I never knew of any time that our pride and joy ever succumbed to sabotage and all the estate would come together in celebration on the 5th of November.

Even though I'd helped with the communal bonfire I preferred to enjoy the family one we had on the back of number 20, it was not as big as the one on the tip but it was mine all mine.

Every house on the street seemed to have their own, it's a wonder none of the houses caught fire.

Once it became dark on the days leading up to Bonfire Night we would leave the sentries to their task of protecting our bonfire; it was now penny for the Guy time.

You'd stuff old clothes with paper and sit it outside the local public house or cinema and ask the general public to hand over their loose change.

Now we had this good idea that we'd just make the head and lay Christopher down and let him pretend he was the Guy, now this worked a treat because we'd only be dragging the head about all night! First off we'd hit the Devonshire public house before getting the early show at the Forum, before running down to the Five Arches and boy were we raking in the pennies.

Next stop was the Forty Foot before getting those coming in and out of the Essoldo on Wordsworth Avenue, but now we were heading into bandit country because the Magnet was on the Southey estate and with us being from Shirecliffe this could result in confrontation, but luckily no one was Guying outside the boozer!

Chris got into costume and lay down like he was dead, and boy was the money coming in our direction.

Unfortunately one drunk thought it would be funny to stick the boot in our Guy and gave it an almighty kick.

You ought to have seen him crap himself when it gave out a scream in pain and shot off minus its head; poor old Chris had copped for a nice boot in the goolies but we thought it was funny!

We went back to dragging a great big stuffed Guy about after that, because no one would volunteer to play it anymore.

Christmas 1963 was ever so special for me, it would be my very first in our own house. I told my dad to make sure that the fire was out when he went to bed, we don't want old Santa burning his arse now do we?

Auntie Dianne had really trimmed the house up and it looked the best ever.

I had got myself a nice Scalextric, it was brilliant, there were four cars and the track was massive.

The box was as big as anything, god knows how old Santa got this down the chimney. With box in hand I rushed over to Grans and set it up on the living room carpet. I was really looking forward to playing with it but I needn't have bothered, within ten minutes I was outside playing on the back garden with my scabby football while the adults were playing at being Stirling Moss, it was supposed to be my Christmas present.

Another great British institution was the pantomime and this year I was dragged along to the Lyceum Theatre to watch Sleeping Beauty with a certain Ronnie Hilton singing about a bloody mouse with clogs on.

I had to sit still for a good couple of hours, while kids were screaming that there was somebody behind him.

I'm not being ungrateful but it was not a patch on the Saturday morning matinee at the local flea pit, no chance of acting the fool and running riot tonight, one would have got a right clip around the old earhole.

I was in the company of the irresistible dynamic duo of Flo and Lily, the menfolk of the family had other and better things to do, Grandad Bill was probably playing snooker in the King's Head, and dad was definitely on the missing list.

Anyway he would have been too busy tarting himself up for another trip to the Black Swan; it was his release from the rigors of grafting all week, and being the greatest single parent in the world.

Dad had been joined by his mates Derek and Arthur, they were off to the town, and looked real lady killers. Once inside the Black Swan, the boys with beer in hand, were looking for the opposite sex. Three such ladies were sat at a table so the three amigos went over for a chat. At first the lads were rebuffed but they were persistent and dad eventually got chatting to this lady called Marie. They seemed to have hit it off and must have chatted all night; Marie was single and lived with her mum and dad on the Manor Estate.

Marie thought he looked a bit like Tony Curtis and that really boosted his ego; he was forthright with her from the off and told her that his wife had left him and his two children a few years previous, they chatted the remainder of the evening before going their separate ways.

I tried my luck at another favourite pastime of kids from our era when we decided to head for the Sheffield Midland Station to try our hand at trainspotting.
I had never been as bored in all my life, writing numbers down in an exercise book; then our day turned for the better when Chammy came running down the platform, it appeared one driver was moving this brand new Diesel-Electric train from one platform to another and he'd welcomed us on-board.
Now this was more like it, having a ride in this Class 45 type engine, the ride must have only lasted about a couple of minutes but it was great.
I told Granddad William when I got home and he was impressed, he'd worked all his life on the railways and he'd never got to ride upfront; mind you when he was a kid I bet it was before Stephenson had built his rocket.
One day not long after we had enjoyed our time at the station Chammy said that my Granddad was pissed up and was staggering up our road.
Now I know he liked a couple after work but I'd never seen my Granddad legless, I rushed to his house but the doors were locked and Gran was not home.
I looked through the front window and saw Granddad slumped in the armchair, he looked completely out of it. I banged on the window but got no response, luckily the catch on the window was faulty and I managed to open it up. Once inside I tried desperately to wake him, the kettle had boiled itself dry and was on fire.
I managed to throw that on the back garden and Granddad was in a right state, Chammy had managed to alert the neighbours and soon the adults had the situation under control.
It turned out that he had not been drinking, his crew had been working in some railway tunnel and it was the fumes from these new-fangled engines that had poisoned them, they had been in this polluted atmosphere all day, and it had affected them greatly.
It was now 1964 and I was well and truly settled in our family home, Auntie Dianne was showing signs of the old fattening of the stomach, but this time, unlike 1960, the soon born to be cousin would not be sharing my bedroom, we had completely downsized from the time spent at number 20, there was only five of us sharing our abode, so the soon to be patter of tiny feet would not burden us too much.
As we were due to welcome new life into the family, I had my very first taste of what it was like to lose someone special, that big armchair in Hoyland Road was now vacant, George Henry had departed this earth, he had been taken at the age of 83, his pipes were still by the fire side, they looked lonely, no more would they be taken outside to create that mystical smoking effect, that had me thinking magical thoughts......
Joanne was born not long after and I looked on her as a little baby sister, I was now 9-years-old and Uncle Fred had for the past few years let me accompany him when he played golf, I loved the times he let me haul his golf clubs around Concord Park.
I remember he gave me a right bollocking for trying to get them out of the car and ended up scattering his prize possessions across the car park.
He must have forgiven me because he spent ages cutting down a set for me, and I'd

bang the odd ball about just like him; mind you when he'd dropped me off at Grans I'd just sling them in the coalhouse and rush in to see what delights she had cooked up. On returning from school one day I was horrified to find that the coalman had been and deposited a dozen sacks of coal onto the clubs that Uncle Fred had painstakingly laboured over.

I know I was not one for knocking that little white ball about but I was mortified that one of my very few possessions was buried under a ton of nutty slack!

Thankfully our Fred never saw what a dozen sacks of coal could do to a bag of clubs - they were in a right state and the bag was torn to pieces.

Fred went on to be quite good at knocking that little ball about, because he managed to win the Banning Cup - a prestigious tournament that was played at Tinsley Park in Sheffield.

He was that good he managed to also win it for a second time, and still plays to a decent standard today.

There was never a dull moment when our lot were around making dens, playing football, and best of all hanging onto the back of the lorries that took the rubbish to the tip.

The drivers would see us in their mirrors emerge from our vantage point and they would slow on purpose to allow us access to their vehicle, then once we'd got a hold they'd try to shake us off while we would hang on for grim death!

This was great until one sadistic bastard thought it would be funny to travel at lightning speed, and boy did he shift.

Kids were being flung everywhere and we were lucky no one was killed.

A few of us had been bloodied so we needed to avenge our injuries. We searched the tip for discarded tyres and boy they were plenty.

We collected them all and placed them on my Grans back garden, and waited in anticipation for the demented driver to pay his next visit.

You ought to have seen his face when our ammunition was heading his way; we must have launched dozens and a couple made direct hits smashing his cab window!

How we screamed for joy and danced a jig until we realised he'd spotted us and had turned his truck around. Kids scattered everywhere and me and Wes only made it to the front of number 16 when his truck crawled up our street.

We were like rabbits caught in the headlights, it was broad daylight and here we were laid in our near neighbours front garden with a demented trucker on our case.

No one was apprehended for our escapade but it taught us one almighty lesson, always plan an escape route if the joke backfires.

I was living life to the full and the only thing that was missing was a bicycle; usually Chris had a spare one in the outside shed but it was rusty and crap, beggars cannot be choosers I suppose.

One day my dad told me to have a look out the back of our house, bloody hell my first bike, and boy did I have a smile as broad as the Wicker Arches.

I could not thank him enough; it must have cost him a week's wages I thought.

Off I shot to the garages on Longley Avenue West, this was our very own racetrack and boy did the kids hurtle around there at breakneck speed.

Chris was there with his elder brother Charlie, "Let's have a go?" he asked, bloody hell I'd only had it five minutes and it's been confiscated.

But boy did Charlie know how to ride a bike; he must have been doing a hundred miles an hour!

Then disaster, he failed to take the corner and bang the front wheel of my new bike was in pieces. Oh shit! My dad must have scrimped and scraped to afford this and look at it. I'd fucked it this time and I could feel my arse starting to glow already, Charles took control of the situation and it was off to the shed at the bottom of their garden.

God it was full of junk but he found what he was looking for; a rusty wheel that had seen better days. Chris came out of the house with a bowl of steaming water and his mother's Brillo Pads and Duraglit.

Within no time at all most of the rust was gone and the silver pads of Duraglit added to the sparkle.

But would it work?

Would him indoors suss out my predicament and tan my arse?

I was fine and he never knew that my first ever bicycle had a surrogate front wheel that had spent most of its life in the dark of Bar-Bars shed, that was the nickname we had given Christopher because of his surname being Bartholomew and he didn't seem to mind.

I loved that bike, I was never off it, we would cycle down to the Rivelin Valley and spend hours larking about around the river.

We were always messing about round water, it was a wonder we didn't have webbed feet, and also we would ride across the meadows to Parkwood Springs.

There was one track there that only the foolhardy would ride down, it was a sheer drop and many a kid had come a cropper at the bottom of that hill.

It was also about this time that cycle speedway was introduced into the city, and Parkwood had their very own track.

When it was not in use we would borrow it for the duration but I was crap at it, I was not brave enough to keep my hands off the brakes and I loved my knees too much.

Christopher was like his brothers in that department he loved circling the track at lightning speed, and if he fell off he'd just dust himself down and get straight back onto the saddle.

There was also another track near the Essoldo picture house on Wordsworth Avenue; it was a popular pastime for the kids of Sheffield 5 and 6.

You could also have fun on four wheels as well, everyone made themselves a trolley or box cart, all you needed was a redundant pram (preferable the ones with great big wheels.)

My Uncle Mick helped me make mine, he acquired the timber from work and Granddad got a great big bolt from off the railways, the back of my racing machine would have two great big wheels fastened to the chassis.

This is where you would sit and the seat off an old kitchen chair would do the business, then a piece of wood at the front would hold the other two wheels.

You would steer it using your feet or piece of string fastened to the axle, once this was spruced up with Gran's finest emulsion you were ready to race.

We had our own personalised race track on the estate; we would race our trolleys from the top of Musgrave Road then turn a sharp left into Longley Avenue West before reaching the finishing line outside the garages.

We always made sure that we had someone positioned to watch for other road users and in those days you hardly saw or knew of anyone who had a car.

This was our very own Brands Hatch, with a bit of luck you could get four abreast at the starting line, some drivers preferred to go down on their stomachs thus holding the axle with their hands, this was only done by the mental or foolhardy amongst us because they could find it difficult to brake in an emergency.

Anyway I cannot really remember who I was racing against but I do know that I was leading as we approached the turn; you ought to have seen my face when the local bus blocked my path!

Where had that bastard come from?

My cart hit the side but I'd jumped clear and boy did my arm hurt, it was bent double, the lads took me to my Grans and she immediately had me off to the Northern General Hospital.

We were lucky that it was within walking distance, and before long I had been put in plaster and boy did it hurt.

That put paid to my schooling for a few weeks!

I was soon back at school and my right arm had mended nicely.

Mind you the collecting of football cards had me on a return visit to the Northern.....

This craze was sweeping the nation, you would spend every spare penny on the damn things, and I think you got five football cards in every packet plus a flat piece of pink chewing gum.

We'd barter and swap every minute of every school day. As soon as the dinner bell had gone and the cards were out.

One card caught my eye, it was Brian Labone of Everton which Wes had in his swaps. Unfortunately for me Glen also needed old Brian, so Wes being the chap he was said you'll have to race for it and first to the school gates gets it.

Well off we shot and it was neck and neck so I decided to leap down the steep banking to gain the advantage, trouble was I mistimed my leap and went head over heels and my newly fixed right arm was in pieces again!

Off to the Northern again and this time I'd done it good and proper, I was in hospital for weeks and at one time the school nurse started to get me to write with my left hand in case the right was fucked up.

Luckily for me, at least I'd done it before I was due to have trials for the school football team.

My mates visited me one school dinner time, which was good of them because I was really down in the dumps.

It didn't stop them nicking my scabby football off the back garden though, the thieving bastards.

The Kids Are Alright

Mischief was the keyword for the Shirecliffe kids and we got up to plenty, but where do I start to remind myself what strokes we pulled?

Well firstly in the cupboard next to the fire, there were these round discs of what looked like pressed tar, with a hole in the middle with the words Beatles and Rolling Stones emblazoned across them.

I'll tell you something they made great skimmers and I knew they belonged to our Mick but he wouldn't miss one or two or three or four.

Another trick the oldies had was putting very small children through the local supermarket window that just happened to be adjacent to the storeroom; goodies would be passed out with the older kids getting the lions share, but there were plenty of leftovers for the ankle biters!

The cinema was the bright light that attracted all the local junior moths every Saturday morning.

The one pictured above was the Forum on Herries Road, we would queue way past the Devonshire public house to gain entry, and now it was my turn after watching them from my pram all those years ago.

We would queue for what seemed like an eternity before they would let us in.

I had raided Gran's pantry and had pockets full of dried peas, along with that was my safely secreted pea shooter.

I would hide it inside my long socks; I was getting on in years and still sported short trousers.

Once the lights had dimmed, all the baddies on the silver screen would be targeted, the overworked staff would be seen dragging kids to the exits, and we would be screaming our heads off.

I was a dead shot and would home in on my intended target, and then a gob full of peas would be heading in their direction!

If the big lads caught you, they would dish out the classic Indian burn, or just bloody your nose.

An avalanche of green missiles would be exchanged all morning, it was our time, no adults to spoil our fun unless the commissioner grabbed you by the throat and booted you up the arse before flinging you through the emergency exit, and your knees would be bloodied after engaging the tarmac.

It was soon over, the lights would be switched on, and hundreds of kids would charge like the light brigade for the exit.

The staff would get their last slaps in until the same time next week, mind it would take them a bloody week to clear up that mushy mess, but did we care, did we, we loved it time after time.

47

You never heard what the likes of Roy Rogers and the Lone Ranger were saying because the noise the kids were making was deafening.

After the film was over we'd head for the tip and re-enact the mornings events, but nobody would ever own up to being shot and fights would break out all over the place.

But my ultimate cowboy hero was Tex Tucker from Four Feather Falls fame, you see he had magic guns that fired on their own and even when all the bad guys had good old Tex cornered his guns would come to the rescue; I tried tying mine up with string but it never had the desired effect.

Another great of the silver screen was the various war films, but these usually had an A certificate which meant you had to be accompanied by an adult.

Now round our way these were in short supply on a Saturday night because they'd be boozing in the Devonshire, Five Arches or like my dad, the Mucky Duck in town.

This never put Wesley and me off, if there was a cracking film we wanted to see.

We'd wait patiently for some kind hearted film buff and utter the immortal words of: "Will you take us in mister?"

We'd have the money but needed an adult to get us through the doors, nine times out of ten this would work and once inside we'd find a nice couple of seats to enjoy John Wayne giving shit to the Japs and Germans.

We'd also be munching our way through a big box of chocolates that we'd found lying in the street next to the local supermarket.

I loved those Saturday nights at the movies; we were a right team, a great double act, the local paper would be scanned, and the movie chosen, long gone was that peashooter and peas, we had grown up; we would sit in silence and hang on every word.

The woman, who dished out those little tickets, gazed in amazement as we changed our adult every week, we must have been the only kids on the estate that changed our guardians on a weekly basis.

But it achieved its aim, and it led me to believe in that age old saying that if you don't ask you certainly don't get.

After it was over we'd dash down to the Five Arches and open the lounge door, and try to grab Gran's attention, scrounge a couple of shillings, and sit on the pub wall and enjoy a bottle of pop, bag of crisps with those little blue bags inside that contained salt. Sometimes the bag included two and if you were not careful you'd finish up with a gob full of salt!

Once Gran and Grandad had surfaced, we would head for the chip shop, and a golden bag of chips with scraps would be heading my way, lashings of salt and vinegar would be administrated and I would carefully blow every chip so it didn't burn my insides.

Saturday, the greatest day of the week. The traditional breakfast down at Uncle Franks which contained bread, tomatoes and relish.

The football if Wednesday were at home, if they were away I would sit with my Grandad and cheer the antics of Billy Two Rivers and Jackie Pallo while they wrestled in front of my very eyes.

Get my tea down my neck while listening to the football results.

Call for Wesley and head for the flicks before finishing off the night with those chips, bloody happy days indeed.

The other great treat the local kids enjoyed was giving Woolworth's a visit whether in town or Hillsborough Corner.

On one such trip with Chammy we'd dipped in and out of good old Woollies a good half a dozen times.

Our pockets filled with crap but it had cost us nothing, unfortunately we tried our luck once too often and got nicked.

Dad was none too pleased that at the age of nine his son had been caught shoplifting, and boy did I get it after he'd had to queue the following Monday with all the other parents down the length of Dixon Lane proving that half the kids in Sheffield were giving good old Woollies a visit.

Another good money spinner was getting into the back yard of the Devonshire or the Five Arches, and retrieving the beer and pop bottles, there was always a couple of pence on them.

So you would bring them back.

We would carry that crate from one boozer to the other, then we would have another crate away and make a return trip up or down Herries Road to repeat the performance. Unfortunately the buggers started stamping and tearing the labels, once they had paid out on them, putting paid to our easy money exercise.

Our good old tip was our Disneyworld, no flying off for two weeks in the sun at some exotic destination for the kids of the 1950s, the best it got was a club day trip where they bunged you a couple of bob, an apple and orange and a bottle of pop.

The coaches stretched the length of the road outside the Pitsmoor Club, all the kids would wave off mum and dad or in my case my Gran as we set off towards the end of the world which I think was in a place called Cleethorpes, it took bloody hours to reach our destination, and my club money was burning a hole in my pocket.

This was around 1965 and could you imagine the sight of a few hundred kids converging unsupervised to a seaside resort near you. We poured off the coaches on the seafront and boy what a dump it was, a shack full of slot machines and a little fair on the beach, my money had disappeared in about five minutes and now we had about four hours to kill before we were treated to a fish supper before we returned home.

Kids were giving the shopkeepers the right old run-around, they did not have the security of places like Woolworth's, so were easy prey for the Shirecliffe shoplifters, we'd sit on the seawall and swap our goodies, well there would be only a certain amount of rock and candy floss these little bodies could consume.

And I thought we were at the seaside, it was about a ten mile walk out over the sands to even get your toes wet. Give me our local tip any day than endure a day like we were enduring.

On the plus side we had been treated well by the club's committee whose job it was to make sure that all the kids got returned safely to the club later on that evening.

Marie, dad's girlfriend that he met at the Mucky Duck, played a blinder one evening when she told my dad to get the kids sorted because it was to be a scorching day the forthcoming Saturday, and that she would treat the three of us to a day out in Blackpool.

We were to meet her at the Midland Station and be whisked off to the seaside, as she waited patiently for us to arrive, wearing a summery blouse, mini skirt and sandals, her face was a bloody picture when we came into view, all dressed in suits.

We are going to the coast, she muttered under her breath, not a bloody wedding, it was roasting, it must have been 100 degrees, and me and our kid, were melting.

This clobber was ok for fleecing the neighbours at Whitsuntide, not very suitable attired for riding a donkey or playing on the sands - these were our very best outfits.

But this was a very special treat, from a very special lady, and dad better get his act together, or he was truly going to miss the boat on this one.

Another time I got anywhere near water in those days was when Uncle Fred and his mate Jack would think it would be great to drag me and our Mark and Jack's two kids all the way to this lake, so they could play with their motorboat.

Well I'll tell you something Freddie boy, it was no fun for us sat on the bank side while you two played like two pirates on the high seas, I'm not being ungrateful but five minutes in the damn thing was the only time us kids got.

Well I tell a lie apart from larking about in the River Don, my Granddad once took me with Uncle Frank on a fishing match that was organised by Padley and Venables, where Uncle Frank worked, and while they stopped off at some café on the way to the river I decided to clamber on top of the wall to climb this tree but fell off and landed in the stinging nettles.

My day was spent on the coach surrounded by dock leaves, I'd been stung everywhere and my skin was red raw, never did get invited again when the grownups went fishing.

The River Don was a right magnet for the estate kids, and we would spend many a happy hour playing along its banks.

Someone once came up with this bright idea that if you followed the river far enough it would lead you to the sea.

So one morning we rendezvoused at the bridge that led you to the speedway stadium at Owlerton, it was bloody tough going this exploration bit, we managed to pass the football ground at Hillsborough but it had took us an age, on we progressed as we reached Winn Gardens near the Middlewood Mental Institution.

We had gone as far as we could, it was decided that we would go home for our dinners and resume this great adventure another day, but we never did make it to the ocean, and our navigational days were over for good.

Football Crazy, Football Mad

August 1963 saw our little gang get ourselves organised to visit Hillsborough for the very first time, the visitors were Manchester United, and I could not wait as we made that short trip down Herries Road.

I was seven, about the same age as my dad when he first watched the Owls back in 1937, but this time there was no war looming to put paid to my Saturday afternoons watching my favourite football team.

The game ended in a 3-3 draw, so I was relatively happy as I ran up to Grans to see what she had cooked for my tea.

My very first programme was carefully placed inside the cupboard next to the fire - others soon followed.

A lesson was learned though, remember those circular pieces of tar that belonged to Uncle Mick, those we would skim to our hearts content?

Well he did find out that we or I had taken a few, in retaliation he burnt half of my precious programmes, well bless him he only burnt 50% of them.

During my first few months of school life, my trips to watch Sheffield Wednesday increased no end, in the run up to Christmas I had seen them play twelve times; they had won on ten games, drawn one and lost only once to Leicester City.

This team of mine were world beaters, I had really picked a great team to support, unfortunately I soon realised they were not very good when they played away from home because they had lost six on their travels.

One Saturday in January 1964 saw us kicking the ball about in our street because Wednesday were away from home.

Stephen Bedell, who lived up the road at number 40 and was a couple of years older than us, suggested that we go to Bramall Lane because the Blades, our bitterest rivals from across the city, were playing Swansea Town in the FA Cup, and they had the famous Ivor Allchurch in their side.

As usual I had no money so I knew for a fact that dad would never fund a trip to that place so I asked him or a couple of bob so I could go and watch the reserves at Hillsborough.

Town was certainly out of bounds for me, so a little white lie would do no harm. With money in my pocket we were off and finished up on the Bramall Lane end with all the Swansea supporters, well we hadn't come to cheer on United had we?

The atmosphere was great and those blokes who talked really funny were brilliant company and the game ended in stalemate, they asked us if we were coming to South Wales for the replay, but that was definitely off the menu. God if my dad knew I'd been to the Lane my arse would be getting well and truly slapped.

We were on a high as we boarded the bus back to Shirecliffe and I must admit we were a bit noisy on the journey home, I rushed to Grans to deposit my first programme from the Lane in the cupboard, and well I didn't want dad seeing it.

Next morning at the breakfast table dad looked in a right good mood and I thought that I had got away with my trip to the Lane, he then asked how the reserves had got on yesterday, and without thinking replied won 2-1, whack! He clipped me around the head. Now that was a shock to the system because I can honestly say I think that was the first time I'd seen and felt him respond in this way.

I'd been found out and while he was waiting for the bus to go into town a neighbour had grassed me up saying she'd seen us acting up on the bus.

I don't think it was the fact that I'd gone to the match, it was the hurt I'd caused by lying to him and boy did I feel the wrath for a couple of days.

I loved football and would spend hours on Gran's back garden, kicking my ball about, even when it went dark I'd run inside and put the kitchen and porch light on and even the upstairs back bedroom just so I could carry on playing into the night.

Who the fuck plays football on their own, not only did I do that but I would recite the teams that had graced Hillsborough the previous Saturday: Springett, Smith, Megson, Eustace, Mobley, Young, Finney, Fantham, Hickton, Ford and Dobson.

Colin Dobson was my favourite player and my dad had got me a blue and white striped shirt which he had stuck two pieces of black tape on the back in the shape of the number 11.

Also he'd managed to get me my first proper pair of football boots, he once bought me some of those that you put the studs in with nails but they would tear my feet to shreds.

We had now been in number 23 for well over twelve months, and I loved our street, loads of kids playing football with the gaps between the privet hedges acting as the goals, our games would only be interrupted by the occasional car and the mardy bastard a couple of houses down.

He would sometimes run out and grab the ball if it landed in his garden, if this happened I would shout Gran who would threaten to remove his arms if our ball was not forthcoming, and it did the trick every time to our amusement.

We would then be told by my Grandma to play on the wasteland at the top of the street, this was ok but if the ball went off the edge it would take us ages to retrieve it.

Smithy then had a brainwave. Why not collect all the discarded oil drums that littered the meadows and place them behind the goal? It took us ages to roll the buggers up that steep incline but boy did it look great when we stacked them two high to the rear of the goal. This seemed to do the trick and many a time the ball rebounded from the drums to keep the game flowing.

With football over for another day it was time for tea, the game always came to an abrupt end when Richard's mother shouted him, you see it was his ball so he decided when we started and finished the game because his was the only decent football for miles around or so it seemed.

The next day all the street kids would twiddle their thumbs and sit on the corsey edge waiting for Rich to come out to play. He always seemed to be the last to get ready and would the bugger let us have the ball - no.

Mind you it was in mint condition and must have cost his dad a hundred pound because it was just like those you saw at Hillsborough.

Once he was out off we shot to our very own Wembley Stadium and our oil drum terrace, but what had happened to our hard work from the previous day? The lot of them had disappeared.

It turned out that the bloke who looked after the site thought it would be funny to roll them back down the valley. He watched us toil all day to get them pitch side from the safety of his hut.

A couple of days later his hut caught fire, I think he'd discarded a cigarette end that he'd forgotten to put out.

Richard Harwood went on to play professional football for Sheffield United while Smithy or Mark Smith played 234 times for Sheffield Wednesday, so that little bit of waste land at the top of Musgrave Road must have been a special place for nurturing the skills needed for the modern game of football.

After making my Hillsborough debut back in 1963, I was football crackers, every minute of every single day I was always kicking a ball about with my mates, or if there was no one to play with, I'd be on the back of Gran's re-living the latest games I had witnessed.

I had also seen the Owls play against foreign opposition when Utrecht from Holland came to Hillsborough, the European adventure didn't last long though because to the annoyance of bomb damaged Sheffield we lost to FC.Koln of Germany.

I had loved my very first season amongst the Wednesday faithful; I had been given an autograph book by my dad, just like the one he had obtained some thirty years previous; it was impossible to work out who had signed it though, unless you could recognize the opposition players that were playing at Hillsborough that day.

I could not wait for those summer holidays to end; well we hardly went anywhere, the odd club day trip to the seaside and a day in the park, but the majority of time was spent larking about on the Shirecliffe tip.

Another great football adventure was the F.A.Cup, not that the Owls had been successful but come the month of March, thousands would descend on Sheffield 6, from all over the country, our little gang would stand on the hilltop that overlooked the stadium and witness the colour change from the normal match day attire of blue and white.

The first two teams to battle it out was the red and white of Manchester United and the claret and blue of West Ham United. Over 60,000 supporters descended on Hillsborough, our little gang had tied our colours to the Hammers from East London, well there was no chance of us supporting anyone who played in the colours of red.

We soon vacated that hilltop because it was pissing it down, the weather was terrible, we moved onto the stadium and it was every kid for themselves.

If you were clever you could attach yourself to a big bloke and when he pushed the turnstile you could squeeze yourself inside and enjoy a free game of football.

The odds on us all getting in was remote to say the least, it was better to wait and bide your time, wait for the crowds to gather, until there was a bit of a crush, I was a skinny little bugger and was being pushed from pillar to post, but I saw my chance and glued myself to the fans of Manchester United, well beggars could not be choosers as they occupied the spion kop.

I had done it, I was in, I rushed to take up my usual position on that concrete ledge but it was impossible to move, it took me an age to reach the front, but I was like a drowned bloody rat, I squashed and squeezed my way through.

The flags that were flying majestically above the North Stand would have been ringing wet, and so was I, whose country they represented was anyone's guess; I wasn't too clever when it came to geography.

The teams came out and Manchester United was wearing white with a red trim and West Ham had a light blue body with two claret bars across their shirts.

The pitch had seen better days, it was like a quagmire, they would have been better off taking the ball and using our pitch at the top of Musgrave Road, but the odds on 60 odd thousand squeezing in would be near on impossible.

I enjoyed seeing the likes of Best and Law take on the soon to be legendary Moore and Hurst, it was an end to end encounter but the first half was without a goal, West Ham were now kicking towards their supporters on the Leppings Lane end and had them in a frenzy soon after the re-start by scoring first, they soon had the Manchester supporters deflated when they made it 2-0.

I felt it best to join in the cheering when Denis Law made it 2-1, but our Hammers won the day when they added another and returned to London in a happy mood.

I was thinking that it would take them an age to return home while I sprinted up Herries Road to enjoy my tea, best keep my little adventure to myself for the time being, and I had also not managed to grab myself a programme, but I'd not got a tanner on me.

I was really piss wet through when I put my head through the door at Grans.

She grabbed me and dragged me over to number 23, and I was thrown in the bath, the old lady was going on about me getting something called pneumonia, apparently it was rife in Manchester and London.

Once changed and dried out, it was back to Grans for her golden brown chips with crusty bread and butter, topped off with Henderson's Relish, what a perfect end to another perfect day, not much chance of going out and playing football tonight, nor was there a cat in hells chance of sitting on the pub wall at the Five Arches until it was chucking out time, my day was over.

Out of our little gang only Wesley had made it inside, the rest had failed miserably, it was a bit of a lottery and our numbers had come up on that occasion but the following year when Manchester United came back to face Leeds United at Hillsborough, I had to sit it out, which was a blessing really because the game ended in a goalless draw, before the team from Yorkshire won the replay and enjoyed a trip to Wembley.

I had now had two full seasons on the terraces of Hillsborough and my team had won a damn sight more than they had lost, but it was on the 30th of March 1964 that I went and sat in the North Stand with my dad, and enjoyed for the very first time that ritual where he hands over that supporting baton to the next generation, that was the very first and last time we enjoyed the football together, it was nice but I missed that bloody concrete ledge with the rest of my mates.

One thing I did notice at such a tender age was that the crowds were now dipping under that 20,000 barrier on a regular basis, what was happening with the football going public, had they had enough of this football going ritual, what else was grabbing their attention on the Saturday afternoon?

The terraces were now being taken over by the kids, the grown-ups were pissing off in their thousands, the kids had now taken over this football asylum, and we were enjoying every minute of it.

The Golden Year of 1966

I was now growing up fast and the school years were flying by, we'd moved on from getting our heads shoved down the toilet, well Chris had anyway. Home life was fine now that we'd established ourselves across the road at number 23, Uncle Fred and Dianne had brought another addition to the household in the shape of a little Labrador puppy they'd brought back from a place called Cornwall.

I loved that little dog even though it used to piss and shit just outside the downstairs privy and one night while wanting a leak I stepped in it, god I nearly threw up.

One day that little dog got out and even though all the kids searched for hours and hours we never did find it, that was the very first time I'd had a pet as such and boy did I miss that little doggie.

Dad was still a regular visitor to the Black Swan and he and Marie had been dating, and seemed to be getting on great until she dropped a bombshell, she told my dad that she could not see him anymore because she was getting grief at home.

It appeared one of her so called mates had told her mother that he was married and had two kids; he was devastated and asked her to reconsider.

He told her that his wife had left years ago, but it made no odds and they parted that evening.

This must have hurt him no end, he was not married, they were doing nothing wrong, technically they were both single, apart from dad having two kids.

Marie went home and told her mother that she had ended her liaison with the family man; her mother said that if she had kept on seeing him she would have brought shame on herself, the family and the Manor.

Marie kept quiet, she just wanted a quiet life, with no family bickering, and this pleased her mum and dad but not her.

Back in the Black Swan she was approached by Derek who told her that Jim was not happy that he had been labelled by people who did not know the full story, he asked her to go with Jim for a quiet drink in the nearby Queens Head so they could chat.

She agreed and when they entered the pub my dad asked her to get the beer in because he was stony broke.

They had a right heart to heart and even thought it was his kids that were putting her off, he even offered to put us into care if she would go out with him, no it's not the kids, I love children, she said it's my mother she thinks what we are doing is wrong.

Marie then realised that dad was serious about her and reluctantly offered to go out with him again; this cheered him up no end and must have skipped all the way home to Sheffield 5.

Marie on the other hand told her mother the story about Jim even offering to put his kids into care if she would go out with him, he cannot do that surely, anyway Marie told her that she was going up to the Shirecliffe to spend the evening with Jim and his kids.

Dad had been backed into a corner, and I never believed that he would give up on us no matter what happened, if he had wanted to get shut of us he could have done it a few years previous but he didn't, he stuck by us no end.

Fred and Dianne had gone out, and they were also looking after Joanne, the evening was great and we liked Marie, just before we were going to bed, my Grandma came across and had a face like thunder.

So this is fucking Marie then, she spluttered, dad immediately sent us to bed. Marie was struck dumb, she had never witnessed language like it in all her life, and was soon getting her coat and heading for the safe haven of the Manor and Queen Mary Crescent. She was nearly in tears when she told her mother the story; it's that area you know, they must be just like your dad's side the Garnhams of the Parson Cross, not like us Perry's from Crookes, we know how to talk and treat people.

Dad's romance was nearly over before it had started, how could this lady get to know our family with Gran raining abuse down on her at any given opportunity, even though her mother was brought up to be polite and see the good in everybody, she was doing her upmost to steer Marie away from Sheffield 5.

Marie though was having none of it, she had not gone through all this hassle to give up on dad just yet, they carried on dating, and enjoyed one another's company, mind you we didn't see much of this because she thought it best not to bring animosity to the family home.

But it was still Grandma who ruled the roost, she would still be our surrogate mother now that the other one was a distant memory, we'd enjoyed yet another day exploring the delights of the tip and boy were we in need of a bath, our Mark was the first to be thrown in and get a good lathering off Gran, now it was my turn to feel the force from the lady who must have been doing this for the past forty years now.

We never had any heating upstairs so when you went to bed it was bloody freezing, thankfully though Uncle Fred had seen fit to carpet all of the upstairs. Gran would quickly dry us and on would go our pyjamas plus the woolliest jumper she could find, our Mark even had a vest underneath all that lot.

Sometimes she would deposit a house brick on the fire, wait until it was red hot, carefully wrap it up in newspaper and place it inside the bed covers, a kind of cemented hot water bottle. On the odd occasion you forgot it was there, you turn over in the middle of the night, and kick the brick.

Off downstairs we shot to be greeted by Marie, she had returned and was waiting for my dad to get ready before they went out on another date.

She was very pleasant, Marie took one look at our night attire and said you don't need all those clothes on to go to bed, so we discarded our jumpers and our Mark removed his vest.

We said our goodbyes and raced up to bed, Gran then noticed that our top layers were missing and insisted that we return to retrieve them before we froze to death, off again we went only to be told by Marie that it was unhealthy to wear all those clothes while you slept and again we returned to Gran minus our jumpers.

Gran was having none of it, and marched downstairs, and she turned the air blue yet again, Marie was speechless as my Gran tore into her, with jumpers and vests put back on we climbed the stairs to bed.

Marie left the house with our dad and we finished up like Scott waiting to explore the Antarctic, the next day Marie told her mother Gertrude about our dysfunctional household and was advised by her mother to give my dad the elbow yet again, but this lass was from the Manor and even though her encounters with Gran would not have been pleasant, we started to see more and more of this lady and apparently she'd taken a liking to my dad.

Dad thought it best to act while the iron was hot and asked Marie to marry him; he didn't want to miss this opportunity for happiness to pass him by, anyway he was 35 now, and that was really old so he

popped the question to the lass from the Manor.

They set the date that on the 22nd of October 1966, she was to become Mrs Cronshaw, but that would have to wait because our football team was making steady progress in this year's FA Cup competition.

Sheffield Wednesday had been going great in the FA Cup, already they had put paid to Reading, Huddersfield and Blackburn Rovers and had reached the semi Finals of the cup for the first time I could remember.

Unfortunately for our gang every game was played away from home so the chance to watch them was impossible to say the least. Our next opponents were to be Chelsea and this was to be played at Villa Park.

One day Uncle Fred asked me to purchase eight tickets for the game; they were only allowing two per person when they went on general sale.

I asked Chris to join me in the queue and after a few hours wait we had four safely tucked away. Why did I not ask Wes and John to join us also, if that had happened then it would have been mission completed?

But I didn't so it was back to the end of this very long line that stretched all the way around the stadium, we were there for ages but eventually returned home to hand over the tickets to Uncle Fred who gave us ten bob each.

The next day at school I was telling all and sundry that I was off to Villa to watch the mighty Owls, boy were the kids jealous and boy was I over the moon, I did not sleep at all on that Friday night.

The 23rd of April will live with me forever, in my excitement I'd never thought to ask if one of the tickets were actually mine, dad must have found it strange that I sat eating my breakfast wearing my favourite Wednesday scarf. Our house started to fill with grownups that I'd never seen before, then Uncle Fred arrived and looked at me and finally the penny dropped, after all my hard work this seemed to be another kid free excursion.

I stood there crying my eyes out when it dawned on me that this little Owl was not part of the plans for the day, well we'll see about that. Off I shot to Grans in such a state she was speechless. I told her my sob story and she was off to confront them.

It turned out they were all going on a coach from the local public house and they were stopping off at some club on the way back.

Gran said that I would understand when I got older why they could not take me, and to make me feel better she said that if Wednesday ever played again in the FA Cup Granddad would take me.

It was alright for them but I had to go out to play and I knew all the kids would take the piss and I was not proved wrong.

Mind you they did bring me a programme back, so at least they were still thinking about me while they were enjoying themselves.

Wednesday did win and come May we would be glued to the television to watch them play Everton in the final.

The day of the match arrived and Gran's house was full to bursting and boy did I wish I was at Wembley.

Before we knew it the Owls were 2-0 up and with only about twenty minutes to go we thought that the cup would be heading back to Sheffield.

How wrong could we be when Everton made the come back to beat all come backs and scored three to win the game 3-2?

After it was all over we replayed the match over and over again on our own little Wembley at the top of Musgrave Road and always Wednesday won the day.

With the domestic football season over until next August the whole country was about to welcome the World because we were hosting the World Cup, and Sheffield had been chosen as one such venue and it was Hillsborough that had received a makeover to make this city proud.

Sheffield was buzzing and Switzerland had taken up residency. All the local kids were drawn towards Hillsborough on the 12th of July to soak up the atmosphere before West Germany played the Swiss, we must have walked around the ground all evening trying to find a way in.

The tournament had kicked off the previous evening when England were held to a 0-0 draw with Uruguay and the football loving nationals were not happy at all.

Unlike the previous evenings bore draw, the Sheffield watching public were enjoying a thriller because those bloody Germans won 5-0, I rushed home to Grans to watch the highlights on the television or goggle box as it was fondly known. Granddad was knocking out the zeds in the armchair after another session in the Kings Head on Commercial Street.

Gran said after you have had your tea Uncle Frank wants to see you. Well my tea disappeared sharpish and I ran down to their house that stood on the corner of Musgrave Road. He was sat having his tea so I waited patiently until he had finished. He then told me to take the envelope off the mantel piece and open it.

I liked Uncle Frank and would visit him for breakfast every Saturday morning while Flo and Lily were in town doing the shopping; he would do tomatoes on toast that were covered in Henderson's Relish, the plate would be licked clean.

I had a biscuit tin that was full of toy soldiers there, one day though I stood on the lid and it sliced into my foot, blood was spurting everywhere and I thought I was going to bleed to death.

I survived though but still bear the scar to this day.

I was now heading for the mantel piece and opened the envelope and pulled out this ticket and started to read it, the words Spain versus Switzerland were emblazed across it and in the bottom corner the price read ten bob.

Uncle Frank had played a blinder and after the disappointment I showed with the Villa Park escapade when they left me sobbing at home; my tears this time were for joy.

The 15th of July 1966 and I was off to Hillsborough to see my very first World Cup match, it was a Friday night and I joined the crowds descending down Herries Road but this time I was on my own personally because none of the gang had got tickets.

I handed over my ticket but this time the programmes were out of my meagre budget.

In through the turnstile and onto my favourite ledge, I think the Swiss were on the Kop but I cannot remember. What I do remember though I had never been as bored in all my life, I'd no mates or team to cheer on, mind you I did see three goals because the Spanish won 2-1.

On the 23rd of July it was the turn of the Germans to re-visit the city where they were to play Uruguay in the Quarter Finals.

Our little gang that included Wes, Chris and John were just messing about as usual in the woods just off Herries Road.

In the bottom was a kind of storm drain that ran under the road and finished up coming out into the fishing pond opposite.

We would dare each other to go inside, at first it was ok because the light behind showed the way but half way through it became pitch black and you had to feel your way in the dark, boy was I glad when you saw daylight at the other end.

Further down the road and under the Five Arches you had the entrance to a great big sewerage pipe that gave off a right stink sometimes; mind you it didn't stop us larking about in it.

At the entrance to the sewer we found a cardboard box that contained hundreds of little flags, we divided them up and headed for the football ground and were only asking for a few pennies for them, but no matter how hard we tried we sold bugger all.

We must have been there a good two hours before the game and eventually we trudged back up Herries Road empty handed in a monetary term but still had these stupid flags that had a white cross on a red background.

We dumped them back from where we had found them; Chris could not understand why the tight arsed Germans and the fans of Uruguay would not part with their money.

How were we to know that it was the national flag of Switzerland?

We were still in junior school and Geography was not one of our favourite subjects.

England had progressed nicely to the Final and there they would meet those tight fisted Germans, again we were crowded round Gran's little black and white television, we had been playing football all morning on the top field but now the streets were deserted.

This time unlike my football team England had done the business and once good old Bobby Moore had lifted the trophy, the kids were back on the street. Rich was dragged out of the house and his replica orange ball just like the one Geoff Hurst had hammered into the back of the German goal was being kicked around on our Wembley.

After the euphoria of hosting the World Cup and the end of the school holidays it was time to start my final year in junior school.

I'd managed to be on the fringe of the school team the previous year and this time around I knew that Mr Spencer would have me in the school goal, our very own Gordon Banks or Ron Springett.

He'd also put four of us forward to represent the school at the trials for Sheffield Boys. We were told by him to arrive at the school on Granville Road on time and handed over our bus tokens, Wesley, John and Glenn Fearn met me at the bus stop on Longley Avenue West and we headed for town.

But this time I was not doing it on the sly and dad wished me all the best.

On arrival the man with the register ticked off all our names and told us to go and get changed; there were hundreds of kids there and far too many goalkeepers, the attitude must have been that this kid was only from Shirecliffe so we will disregard him without seeing him play.

I did manage to play but I joined my mates playing at full back and I was like a fish out of water, we never even finished the game before we were all dragged off.

We were not happy as we headed home, those stuck up bastards that ran the show were really anti-council estate kid, or so we thought.

Monday morning at school Mr Spencer was none too pleased by our treatment, and especially that I'd not even played in goal.

A few weeks later I was summoned into his office and was told that I had been watched playing for the school team and was being included in the squad to represent the city.

To be honest though I spent most of the time sat on the bench and only started one game, I didn't really feel part of the furniture but the goalkeeper made me feel welcome, all the kids were dressed to the nines in their school uniforms and had the best football boots of the time and my Timpson Shooting Stars looked rather shabby.

I was steadily heading towards my eleventh birthday and our Mark was now 6 years of

age and he too had started his school life.

Gran had now realised that my dad had asked Marie to marry him and she had accepted.

She saw this as a threat to her domain and was not too keen on the idea, mind you it would have been nice for me and our kid to enjoy a normal family upbringing.

I was not being ungrateful to my foster Grandmother but it would be nice to have a proper mum and dad for once in our short lives.

Marie, aged 27, was the eldest daughter of Samuel and Gertrude Garnham who were married in 1937; she was born two years later in 1939 and had a younger sister Patricia at 24 and a brother David at 22.

Samuel and Gertrude had lived in Wentworth Street with

Gertrude's father. Her father lived in the attic while her sister Marjorie slept on the landing, Marie spent most of her early life sleeping in a drawer; it was open though.

They then got offered a house of their own on St Phillips Road, but it needed decorating. Gertrude would not move in until the place was clean and tidy, it took Samuel a week to get the job done.

He then borrowed a hand cart to put on their worldly goods and made they short trip to their new home.

What a shock they got when they turned the corner to see their home reduced to rubble, it had been bombed during the night.

With their new abode out of action, they now turned their attention to a nice little one up, one down on Addy Street which is pictured above.

It seemed to have been second time lucky because everything went well with the move, it was now 1940 and the city was not just under attack from the German bombs but tuberculosis was rife amongst the populous of Sheffield.

Samuel had been struck down with the illness and was gravely ill, Marie was also a regular visitor to Winter Street Hospital because she had suffered a mild strain of the virus.

Over the following 12 months the city council and health authority operated a kill or cure policy and transferred those with the disease to a new housing estate that had been built on the Manor.

This estate was so high up overlooking the city that the wind would bite through you but the air was fresh and clean.

This seemed to have done the trick with Samuel, he was getting better with every day spent on these windswept streets, much so, that by 1943 two further additions were added to the Garnham family in the shape of Patricia and David.

Mum had a good upbringing and was well loved and cared for.

She enjoyed her school years at Prince Edwards School, it was during this period that she had a run in with her mother and she was told that she couldn't go out to play.

This really upset her and in a fit of temper, she grabbed a small case and stuffed some clothes into it.

Then she took a chocolate cake her mum had just baked - she was leaving home.

Patricia decided to join her and soon they were making their escape. Unfortunately Pat only got as far as the garden gate before she burst into tears, mum though carried on regardless and made for the wooded area just off Queen Mary Road. That was it now, she was all alone and thinking about her next move. She lasted a couple of hours before she returned just in time for tea, her mother welcomed her back with a couple of smacks to the legs, before washing mum's chocolate covered clothes and cleaning the suitcase.

At the age of nine and seven respectively Marie and Patricia were just not old enough to flee the nest just yet.

My brand new family in waiting, Samuel Garnham the head of the household with his loving wife and my soon to be Gran.

From being motherless for the past few years, I was to be getting not only a mother but another set of Grandparents making three in total. Well I bloody deserved it for what

I have had to put up with over this turbulent period, the added bonus was that I was also to get two more Uncles in the shape of John who was married to Auntie Patricia, my soon to be mothers sister, and not forgetting their brother David, this would be a right bonus come Christmas 1966.

Our school football team pictured below, how I ever kept goal in that big thick jersey, my teammates were Ian Boot, Raymond Carlton, John Gallagher, Geoffrey Bingley, Stephen Canter, Glenn Fearn and Wesley Haywood.

We enjoyed ourselves playing for the school team, I don't think we ever won any trophies during this period, but we only had one year at it before we moved onto the senior school.

On the day of the wedding that was to be held at the church on Prince of Wales Road on the Manor, I was representing the school team in a six a side tournament. We did ok but did not win it, dad was in attendance to make sure I didn't abscond and bugger off to play with my mates.

I was dragged back home and slung into the bath, he had to do the honours this time because my Gran was not well and was confined to her bed.

The rest of the day went like clockwork and just after 3pm, Marie Garnham became Marie Cronshaw and we had got what we had hoped for, a mum that would stick by us for the duration.

Mind you it nearly didn't happen because dad had never bothered to seek a divorce, so they had to place an advertisement in the local Sheffield Star and the Daily Mirror.

The powers that be granted him a special licence so that the wedding could go ahead, and I was wondering if Marie really knew what she was letting herself in for.

The reception was held at the Prince of Wales on Derbyshire Lane, this was at the posh end of town and all the kids played happily outside until it got too dark.

The next morning we were up bright and early to enjoy our first family breakfast together.

Unfortunately Uncle Fred had taken the kitchen furniture away with him to his new abode, but who cared we had a woman in the house and this time she was not being borrowed like my

Grandma and Auntie Dianne, she was ours, our mum. I'd not uttered those words for a very long time and to tell you the truth I had a problem spelling the damn thing.

I must have smiled all day as I was out and about on the estate, and another thing that also brightened up my day was that my Gran was back on her feet.

Uncle Fred had moved to his very own house on Herries Road, mind you he did take all the carpets from upstairs, plus the rest of the furniture that belonged to him.

Our house did look sparse as the newlyweds moved in; Marie had kitted out the marital bedroom with a brand new bed, wardrobe, dressing table and chest of drawers.

Fred had left our single beds that he had kindly bought for us, downstairs we had a three piece suite and tiny television, while in the kitchen we still had the old twin tub for doing the washing but the table and four chairs had vanished.

Mum decided that the house needed a makeover and with money in short supply, well I mean they'd borrowed £20 off my Granddad Sam to pay for the wedding photographs, on the understanding that my dad cashed in his insurance policy to pay him back.

So off they went to Blaskeys on Angel Street, to purchase some paint, and while they were in town they made a beeline for Mr Swycher's shop on West Street and thought about splashing out on a new dining table and four chairs plus two rugs for the bedrooms upstairs.

They walked into the shop with their shopping list and dad was very confident that Mr Swycher would do the business, he had been a regular customer for some years now and never fell behind with the re-payments.

Dad was none too pleased when he produced this ledger that had my dad in debt to the sum of just under £300, Marie could not believe it as she surveyed the list of items bought; Valour Velvet curtains, rugs of various sizes, bedding, bedroom furniture and various smaller items.

Marie had seen what we had got first hand and there were no nice posh curtains hanging from our windows, somebody had taken my dad to the cleaners, because they had even bought a sweeper and he was footing the bill.

Marie took control and told Mr Swycher that she would settle the outstanding debt if she could have a copy of all the previous purchases, this he agreed too plus he let them have the table, chairs and rugs.

My mum made him separate the two accounts so she could get to grips with the situation, the following week we enjoyed our first ever family meal in our family home, with my very own family.

It turned out that Grandma Florence had been busy shopping and poor old dad had been footing the bill.

My dad getting married had put a stop to him paying Gran to look after us. Marie had certainly gone and thrown a spanner in the works before the outstanding debt could be settled. We were oblivious to this, but it affected us badly, Gran had also taken money out of our pockets because the money coming in, was not meeting the money going out.

Dad decided to keep Gran's misdemeanour a secret for the time being after all what would he have done without my guardian angel for all those years?

Mum on the other hand was none too pleased about the situation but played along for the time being.

She also still had to pay her father the money they had borrowed for the photographs but it was proving difficult to locate that insurance policy.

It all exploded one morning after we'd gone to school, mum was on her knees cleaning the fire when Gran paid a visit. Where is he she demanded?

I'll tell you where Jim is he's doing a 24 hour shift because we need the money. Oh! Gran replied, he'll bloody work now she spouted.

You see that after his wife left, dad went off the rails a bit.

He had got finished by his employers at Hatfields because he was taking too much time off, and spent time at the mercy of the social security department.

During that period dad couldn't be arsed to register to vote in the general election, and being a staunch Labour supporter like the rest of Sheffield I found this hard to believe.

The Manor lass was having none of it and let rip, yes he's working to pay off the debt that you have landed us with, and we are finding it increasingly difficult to make ends meet.

Gran suddenly burst into tears and that ever present hard exterior started to crumble, mum went into the kitchen and made them both a cup of tea.

The two women sat face to face at the table and Gran opened her heart to my mum.

Firstly she told of her visits to Mr Swycher and the temptation to receive easy credit was just too much, and anyway dad was footing the bill, a new fitted carpet, curtains, a nice kitchen table and bedroom furniture the bill was in the hundreds.

If that was not bad enough she had even cashed in my dad's insurance policy, Gran promised to be back later with the £20 that my parents owed to Granddad Sam.

After all the earlier animosity between the two ladies this bonded them ever closer together. She told my mum that it would be sorted one way or another.

My birthday had come and gone, and I think this was the first time I can remember that I had a card that was from mum and dad, we now moved towards our first ever Christmas as a proper family.

I was wondering what Santa would be bringing my way, our house was well trimmed up and a brand new Christmas tree sat proudly at the side of the roaring fire. How good was this sat watching our very own television with mum and dad, even though the screen was about the size of a beermat.

Our Fred had gone and taken his massive one to Herries Road, why didn't dad go over to Gran's and confiscate theirs?

Anyway, he'd probably paid for it.

School was moving on nicely as we moved into 1967, my very last year in the junior school, and the thought of taking the 11 plus examination would see if you were clever enough to enjoy a Grammar School education at Chaucer School or if you failed it was Shirecliffe Senior School.

On the football front I'd travelled to Scunthorpe, Doncaster and Barnsley with Sheffield Boys but as usual I was just keeping the bench warm.

Mind you on the 25th of March 1967 we entertained Nottingham Boys and after the game we were treated to a meal at Hillsborough before watching Nottingham Forest beat my beloved Wednesday 2-0; we all sat together in the North Stand but I'd have preferred my usual perch on the Kop.

Our school team was great to be involved with and I would love travelling around the city on a Saturday morning, Mr Spencer would hand out the bus tokens on a Friday afternoon and we would congregate at the school to travel together the following day.

After one away trip we were heading down Waingate to catch the bus home when most of the lads invaded Woolworth's, I told them that I would give it a miss and received some stick off them.

Boy was I glad that I'd gone home alone because all the kids were missing from school Monday morning because they were lined up with their fathers on Dixon Lane, and getting ready to meet the store manager.

But it was not just football that I was good at, I loved swimming and was awarded a free year's swimming at Sutherland Road, but it was the lifesaving certificate that nearly drowned me, we were told to bring a pair of pyjamas for our test.

Like an idiot I brought some that you took off over your head, when it was my turn, I jumped in and swam towards the deep end, once there you had to remove your clothing, the bottoms were not a problem, but could I not get the top off, I kept going under but would not give up.

The instructor reached out with a pole but I would not grab it, again and again I struggled to get the top off, all the lads were laughing and the teacher was none too pleased. In the end I reluctantly packed it in and when those certificates were handed out, I missed out. I did go onto represent the school at the Sheffield Swimming Championships at Hillsborough Baths, but because I was dire at diving I trailed well behind the winner, but I'd gave it my best shot.

Wednesday were again making steady progress in the FA Cup. They were at Stamford Bridge to meet Chelsea, I rushed to Gran's and reminded her what she had said the previous year and would she ask Granddad to take me, now he was more likely to be found in the Kings Head most Saturdays at 3pm and not on the terraces of some football stadium, Gran said she would ask him and see if he would take me.

When he came home from work at first he said no way was he going to the football but after realising how disappointed I was last year when they left me sobbing at home he relented and on the 8th of April we travelled by train to London, my first ever away day and there were thousands travelling in support of the Owls.

Granddad must have been the world's worst football supporter because we ended up on the Shed which housed all the Chelsea supporters, I really enjoyed the match and my blue and white did not look out of place amongst all the home fans.

Unfortunately for me and my Granddad Wednesday lost to a very late goal and that was the end of our cup dreams for another year.

I'd really enjoyed my day though and I think Granddad had as well, I had the biggest bag of peanuts to enjoy on the return journey and there were shells everywhere when I'd finished.

I was still enjoying my schooling and my social life was great, it was never a dull moment with my mates.

We loved the so-called burning tip, aptly called because they would deposit the burning embers from the nearby power station.

We loved larking about on that tip and if you were to dig deep enough it would get very warm indeed, and bring a glow to your feet.

We finished the school year and I had failed my exams and it was the Senior School for me, we had visited the place to have a look around and it was massive, and those toilets were big enough to get five heads down.

We were now enjoying another six weeks off school and the summer of 1967 was to be our last before we made the big step up to start our secondary education.

Rumour spread that lorry after lorry were dumping coal onto the tip, apparently they were excavating High Street in the city centre and they had hit a seam of coal, the council were constructing the infamous Hole in the Road and decided to dump all the crap in our neighbourhood.

Chris and I borrowed two dustbins and filled them with coal, we dragged them around the neighbours selling their contents for a few shillings, we worked our bollocks off all day and were as black as the ace of spades but we'd made over a pound between us.

When we were depositing the bins back Chris's dad asked what we had been doing, we told him that we had been flogging coal to the neighbours and he offered to look after our finances so we would not fritter it away.

How gullible were we, once we'd buggered off he was off like a shot to the Five Arches to drink and smoke away our hard earned cash, we were not happy bunnies when we found out so marched across to his small holding and let half of his chickens go free.

The poor old vagrant who frequented the area got the blame and Chris's brothers dished out retribution on the poor old man.

After this the brothers made the allotment more secure and we helped them, I was busily painting away and got too close to old Charlie when he was swinging the hammer and whack, I had a right lump on my head and there was blood everywhere.

We rushed to their house and his mother, god bless her, caked my head in butter. Why did they do that? Was it some kind of miracle cure to heal all ills?

They also kept pigs on their small holding and every Sunday afternoon we would drag our cart around the neighbourhood collecting all the leftovers from the Sunday dinner, and boy did it stink when we added the pig supplement and water. Mind you it didn't pong as bad has those piggies, I hated the buggers and they scared me no end but he was a mate so I helped him out with his weekly chore.

Happy Families

July 1967 saw my mum put on the kind of weight that the other one had in 1960 and I knew this time what was coming. On the 24th of August we witnessed the birth of my baby brother David, well mum and dad did, me and our Mark was left with Gran.

Our David was only about a month old when dad received an official looking letter, it was from a solicitor in Blackpool.

Apparently he had a relative who had recently died and he was the sole heir to her estate. Mum was really excited and envisaged us uprooting the family to spend the rest of our days by the seaside. Dad on the other hand dismissed it straight away, he was not even going to visit the solicitor to see what was on offer.

This lead to an almighty row and mum handed me and our Mark money to go to the pictures. Once we were out of earshot she let rip, I cannot believe you are not even considering making this trip.

I cannot just take time off work to chase a dream he told her, that was it she placed our David in the brand new pram her mother had purchased for her and shot out of the door. She headed for the Manor to be with her mother; Gertrude was a bit taken a back when her daughter waltzed through the door. What's up she queried? Its him mum, he has received this letter from Blackpool about an estate he is entitled too and he won't get off his fat arse and take a look.

Well you cannot stay here, what do you think those two kids are thinking, another mother has done a bunk? She needn't have worried though because after dumping us with Auntie May, dad had followed her up to the Manor.

Dad had relented and would ask for time off work, so they could go to Blackpool; they travelled home that evening to make plans to make that journey to see the solicitor in Blackpool.

They had borrowed another £20 off Granddad Sam to finance their overnight stay and travel expenses. They had caught the first train available, while Auntie May sent us off to school before seeing to our David.

Once they had booked into the guesthouse, they made the visit to the solicitors. He handed them a key and a piece of paper with the old lady's address on. It turned out that the old lady had worked in the nursing profession all her life and had never married.

Mum and dad were told what buses to catch to get to the said property, once they had alighted the transport; they walked down tree lined streets, great big houses stood to attention. Mum quipped that the kids would love living here, how her dreams were shattered when they entered the property. It stank of cat piss, and nothing of real value was left inside the house. Somebody had been inside before them, you do not work all your life and not treat yourself to some nice home comforts, pictures had been removed from the walls; but what other goodies had done a disappearing act?

The local rag and bone man was commissioned by the solicitor to empty the remainder of the property, mum was none too pleased that all he offered them was a take it or leave it £20; they left the house with the solitary £20 and nothing else, no memento, nothing. Once back at the solicitor he told them that the property was rented, and his relation had died penniless.

They must have been gutted as they returned home with just enough money to pay back Granddad Sam. Never mind I probably would have hated spending my days in a great big mansion that was situated in the leafy streets of Blackpool.

Our finances were now being really stretched, dad was the only breadwinner and he seemed to be at work seven days a week.

He had now left the Sheffield Gas Company and moved to a better paid job at Firth Browns, the money was only slightly better but the overtime was great, you see the plant operated 24/7 and his crane had to be manned all the time, so if his mate failed to take him off, he could stay on for another eight hour shift; we hardly ever saw him.

Grandma and mum had really got close and she would always introduce her as her daughter in law. When our David was a few months old Gran asked her if she wanted to help her and Lily clean the Five Arches. Mum asked her friend Auntie May, as we called her, if she would look after our kid for a couple of hours every morning, and she jumped at the chance to be left at home holding the baby.

Mum once complained that she always had to clean the toilets while Flo and Lily sorted the Lounge and Taproom respectively.

She was not being ungrateful and the £4 a week came in very handy, money was much needed but having your hands down a bog seven days a week must have been heartbreaking.

The following week Gran took her concerns on board and switched the duties of my mum and Lily, and while they walked towards the boozer Flo handed a carrier bag to my mum and said once she'd cleaned the Tap Room she was to deposit a couple of bottles of Pale and Brown ale into it and don't forget the nuts and crisps for the kids, mum immediately returned the carrier to Lily and carried on cleaning the toilets.

Mum would be a regular visitor to number 20 and always find time to enjoy a cuppa with my Gran. This particular day my Grandparents had just finished off a nice fish dinner; you ought to have seen my mum's face when Gran scraped off the leftovers into the bin then, without cleaning the plate, placed pastry over it before filling it with apples and telling mum to tell the kids that there was a nice apple pie going into the oven when they get home from school.

We always went to see Gran straight from school and boy did that pie smell good, mum told us not to have any because it would spoil our tea, did we listen, did we buggers.

One day I was left to my own devices while the rest of the family went to see my Grandparents on the Manor, I had Chris round our house and we played football on our back garden and when he left he also took with him the money my mum had left out for the milkman and I got a right shock when dad accused me of having it away. I know I had been a bad lad sometimes but pinching off my very own family was certainly off limits.

Chris had let me down and he knew it but I forgave him and we remained firm friends. Once we travelled to town and got into a spot of bother in a park off Barnsley Road and a gang of kids attacked us and ripped Chris's trousers.

We had decided to walk and save the bus money, I can remember it was freezing and I had to lend him my sheepskin coat in return for his little jacket, we never did venture into that park ever again.

In December 1967 on a visit to Hillsborough, myself and my trusty sheepskin again got into a spot of bother. I'd just paid to get into the Kop when a group of kids came running towards the turnstiles. They were trying to get out of the ground while I was trying to get in. I thought surely we are not that bad that they have decided to ask for their money back. This was to be my first introduction of football violence, these lads were Manchester City fans who had tried to infiltrate the Wednesday end. The Sheffield Boot Boys, as they had been labelled, had sussed them out and were chasing them out of the ground. I on the other hand was struggling to get in, the Wednesdayites must have thought that I had come from Manchester and I received a few digs and slaps. Fucking hell, I'm only 12 years old yet I'm getting what can only be called as friendly fire, my nose was bloodied and my face bruised, why had I left my Wednesday scarf at home? If I'd have been wearing it, the lads would have realised that I also was an Owls supporter. My dad was none too pleased that I had been attacked after I returned home after Wednesday had drawn 1-1 with City.

He even considered stopping me from going to the match. This I was not happy with because I was in danger of missing Wednesday play.

Our Mark was now tagging along with us as we got up to mischief; it was the time of the year that the estate would be overrun with baby pigeons.

We thought it would be great to grab a few and bring them up ourselves, the bestest climbers would be up the drainpipes and before we knew it our cage would be full to bursting with our pedigree racing birds.

We'd managed to get four young chicks and they looked the business, but they would need feeding so off we went; we walked over the Meadows before calling in at my Grans on Hoyland Road.

No drinks of pop in those days, just a nice glass of corporation wine that the local folk called water.

Across the bridge at Neepsend it was rumoured there was two dumped Ghurkha knives. His parents had apparently told him to get rid of them by throwing them into the River Don before he got into trouble.

We climbed Wood Street before turning right into Langsett Road. The bell on the door rang as we entered Mr Horsfall's shop. He was the local corn merchant where myself and Christopher would purchase the feed for their families live stock.

But this time we were not buying in bulk and carrying home on our box cart or trolley cart, we only had a few shillings that we had scraped together, and we didn't get much top quality pigeon feed for our thoroughbred racing machines.

On the way back we even stopped off at the lofts on Penistone Road to ask advice from the old timers whose pigeon lofts looked like stately homes or castles majestically overlooking Penistone Road and the River Don.

You cannot get those wild flying rats to fly and return they laughed. What did they know? We were just starting out in this racing game and they all looked the same to us. Anyway, we were experienced in this field, so we would show them.

We decided that our cage needed tarting up after viewing what they had done, so the kids were sent onto the tip to see what they could find; it was just like bonfire night as loads of timber was heading our way.

This time we were not burning it, we were building with it. We levelled the ground behind Grans house and placed some old wooden doors to make a platform - well we needed somewhere to sit and watch our pigeons fly up into the sky. We also needed to build the cage higher to keep them out of the reach of those neighbourhood cats.

We spent every single minute of every single day looking after those birds; we even covered the cage up with blankets at night to keep them nice and warm just in case there was a chill in the air.

We even decided to decorate our miniature loft, so kids went in search of some lovely nice white paint. We'd managed to cop for a load and began beavering away to our heart's content.

Then disaster struck. Someone knocked a tin over one of our mates, he was covered in it and got really upset. We knew why, his mother was not very nice, she would sometimes lock him in the coalhouse while she went about her business.

We once told Gran about his predicament. She really did not want to get involved physically but knew of a solution. Just get hold of their coalhouse key she told us. Once we had it in our grubby little hands she passed it onto Granddad and told him to get another one cut on his way home from work.

It worked a treat and every time she would deposit him in the coal bunker, like a little Houdini he would escape. Mind you we had to put him back before she returned home. What kind of mother does that to her son? Yes an evil one. We rushed him over to ours and my mum took one look at him and knew she had to do something to stop him getting a good thrashing when she returned home.

She threw the little bugger in the bath while rummaging through a pile of our Mark's clothes, and then she took turpentine to his shoes to remove the remaining evidence that could land him in big bother.

Mum had played a blinder and his mother had not even noticed that her son had returned home in different attire from when he had left the house some hours previous.

He was the same age has our Mark and would spend many a night sleeping at ours, I looked on him as another extension of the family, and he loved stopping at ours.

The pigeons had grown now and we believed it was time to release our world beaters on their maiden flight. How they flapped their wings in anticipation of being set free, one after another they were released and set off like the wind. They were now in full flight and circled above us, over the roof tops then disappeared, no matter how hard we rattled that tin of corn, those ungrateful bastards never did return home.

My time was now over in junior school and I'd moved up to the seniors and all my mates had failed their 11 plus and avoided a trip over to Chaucer School.

I looked the business in my new school uniform. The big school, as it was named, was amazing; the classes were well regimented, and we were back to square one in the pecking order.

These toilets were that big you could probably drown two kids at a time, the Headmaster welcomed us during that first morning assembly. New kids had been shipped in from Southey and Longley junior schools, but most of the kids stuck with their mates who had been by their sides for the past five years.

Huddles of first years congregated on that playground at the mid-morning break, again no one moved towards those toilets. We were like little penguins with that black blazer, white shirt and school tie, while all around we were being eyed by what can only be described as the school pack of killer whales.

Then it suddenly happened, the big fat whales made their move and kids were being dragged off to meet their watery grave, we listened from the outside as the little penguins got their heads shoved done the bog, flush after flush could be heard.

I was again one of the lucky ones. I had reached dinner time dry as a bone, and enjoyed my very first school dinner. I had also not been press-ganged by the big lads. If they got you on their table you would hardly be dished anything up, and forced to wait for any extras that were going begging.

All the food came in metal containers on a tray, the biggest and hardest lad would get first pick. His plate, the greedy bastard, would be overflowing. Then his mate would have second go until the poor old first year was actually scraping the barrel and before he had even finished his measly portion he would be told to queue for any extras that were going begging.

That very first week was an eye opener, I loved the art classes, science and those Bunsen burners, geography and history, while that first game of football in P.E. got yours truly in the school team.

Maths and again the religious nut had me staring out of the class room window which resulted in me getting the board rubber heading my way and it bloody hurt.

We had just about survived the first week unscathed but some of the lads were complaining that their dinner money had been confiscated; five days' worth of slop had been lost forever, the big lads had been confiscating it and spending their ill-gotten gains on cigarettes.

This was out of order so our little gang planned revenge, this we did by singling out one individual; he was a right bully, and the worst in the entire school.

One kid had dared bring his caseball to school and it was commandeered by the bully and his mates; they had booted us off the playground and while we sat on our arses twiddling our thumbs they re-enacted the World Cup Final.

Their blazers made great goal posts and the pitch looked impressive, they were so enthralled in the action they never noticed the gang had secreted a few inkpots in their pockets.

We were long gone before the whistle went for full time. Their faces were a picture as we viewed ink was dripping all over. They were not happy at all. The kid whose ball they had borrowed got a few slaps and kicks and ran off crying, minus his ball.

It was decided from then that school dinners were off the menu, and we hid our dinner money and made for the chippy every day and sat in the woods eating our dinner.

Another first for me was the cross country run just before the first school autumn break. All the school would go on that annual run, the circuit was daunting; one lap of the school field before heading for the woods. Some of the boys opted for their football boots but I choose my plimsolls. We raced on top of that cliff that overlooked the Wednesday ground before crossing the white bridge, up and over before navigating that zigzagging chicane that scared us no end when returning during the dark from the speedway.

The long run by the River Don led to dodging the graves in the local cemetery, up and over the black bridge before coming full circle and ending up sprinting past the prefabs, only one more lap of the fields before the welcoming finishing line.

I had achieved my objective and finished top five in my year, I cannot really recall in what position I finished in the entire school but I was bloody chuffed.

I went on to represent the school but my running attire was not perfect, it was either football boots or plimsolls depending on the weather, football shorts and shirts weighed a bloody ton when wet.

I can remember that very first meeting in Concord Park. Our boys eyed up the opposition, the kids from all the posh schools had running vests and shoes that had spikes instead of studs, and they had a bloody unfair advantage.

It was totally disheartening, we looked a right rag bag outfit, most of us finished right off the pace, except for a lad whose name has been lost forever, that diamond finished well up in the order and he ran in football boots, what would he have done if provided with the right equipment?

We even visited Suggs and asked about those spikey shoes, but they cost a small fortune and they could not be lifted because the clever bastards only ever put one on display.

So my cross-country days were over. what was the point? It was like playing football against the posh kids, but the council boys had to wear carpet slippers. They had such an unfair advantage and it hurt like hell.

All the school were split into four houses which consisted of Australia (yellow) Canada (blue) New Zealand (green) and South Africa (red), I was a Canadian for the duration; throughout the school year you would compete at all different sports such as football, cricket, rounders, plus the girls enjoyed hockey.

This would come to a head when all the school would enjoy the sports day and every kid would have to do there bit, all the big bloody Canadians would be shaking their fists at all the youngsters, making sure they put in a world beating performance, and woe betide anyone who came in trailing behind those Australians, Kiwi's and African's.

I liked school and even managed to play one of the Three Kings in the local nativity play, I looked rather dashing in mums blue quilted dressing gown. My mates thought I was a bit of a Nancy boy for enjoying theatre as it was called.

But I loved the theatre group and the teacher's enthusiasm, and would attend after school, the class would put a play on once a year and I envisaged playing a starring role.

But that would have to wait because Father Christmas was once again heading for number 23 Musgrave Road, but now we were a family of five with the addition of baby David.

He would be taking a cut of the Christmas giving budget, but he was only four months old and not yet really a threat in the annual receiving of present's department.

I was now twelve and my expectations had increased, but unlike kids today you had no idea what would be waiting under that tree come Christmas morning.

We sat there on the eve of Christmas, our eyes glued to the goggle box that was serving up good old family entertainment. After watching some students belt out some hymns and Christmas carols we enjoyed half an hour of Steptoe and Son, and then it was time for bed.

I was none too happy that he would be here in just under five hours and dad had got that fire roaring away; poor old Santa must have got an arse made out of asbestos to withstand that heat.

I thought to myself that I had been a good boy in 1967, I had not been naughty in the shoplifting department, and I was enjoying my schooling and helping around the house, and going on as many errands that my mum wanted.

The following morning we were up like a lark, we had only been bloody waiting since four o'clock to be given the green light and get out of bed, dad had been up to get the coal fire started with us having a baby in the house, mum made us have our breakfast before we got anywhere near that Christmas tree.

After breakfast had been demolished in about sixty seconds it was into the front room, David was in his high chair; just like me in 1955 and our Mark in 1960.

This time though mum had taken over the mantle of chief dishing out of presents coordinator, and we had the added bonus of an extra set of grandparents showering us with gifts plus another auntie and uncle in the shape of Patricia and David.

My pile was mounting by the minute and by this rate I would be for the first time in my life reaching double figures, I was also like every other kid in the country, opening the smallest present first and leaving the big ones until last.

So here goes: a nice new pair of football socks, a selection box, and some nice socks for school (how practical), another selection box, a football annual, a pair of school trousers, another selection box, Beano annual, a lovely knitted jumper, and another lovely knitted jumper.

Just two to open and my mind is racing; what had I kept for the crowning glory? What goodies were still lurking under the layers of wrapping paper? They were both from mum and dad, I might ditch the presents and just keep the paper that said from mum and dad on.

That was my greatest gift having a mum and dad and a new baby brother. You can keep your mountains of selection boxes, well on second thoughts they have got my name on, and it would be an insult to return them.

They had done the business, a brand new pair of football boots and a caseball, and it was orange in colour, it must have cost dad a month's wages.

Christmas day and on go the socks, and I dig out my shorts and shirt, I'm now dressed for the occasion, with my new boots, the bees knees, with ball tucked under my arm, I'm off to Grans, my own personal Hillsborough.

The pre-match nerves are starting to bite, I get a clip for walking into her house with my football boots on, but I know what I am looking for, it's the match day programme from the previous game, bloody hell it's only West Ham United.

Wednesday would be up against it today, this lot included Moore, Hurst, Peters plus Bonds, Lampard and Brooking plus a bloke called Redknapp.

The Owls lined up with Peter Springett, he had replaced Brother Ron, Smith, Megson, Mobley, Ellis, Young, Whitham, Fantham, Ritchie, McCalliog and Branfoot.

There are 24,003 crammed onto Gran's back garden and we are underway. Today I am big John Ritchie and these boots are working wonders because I open the scoring to the delight of the watching faithful which in reality are Gran who is at the window preparing the dinner and our Mark who is the West Ham goalkeeper.

Soon Ritchie makes it two to the Owls, following on from a great strike by Fantham, Mark is having a nightmare, and this seven year old is just no match for the mighty Owls.

Half time and we break for a drink of water. Mark tries to escape back to the sanctuary of number 23, but I drag him back for the second half, I appease him by letting him take a penalty to make the score Sheffield Wednesday 3 West Ham United 1.

But it's to no avail because Whitham cracks in number four and the game is well and truly over.

We trudge back home and we both get slung into the bath, our kid is in a right state, he'd only gone and muddied his clothes, what had he been doing to get in such a state? We thought it best to keep her in the dark for the time being, didn't fancy another clip on Christmas day; we both scrubbed up nicely, and tucked into our dinner, a nice piece of pork was the offering, well only the bloody posh people could enjoy the delights of a turkey.

This was my greatest ever Christmas, after such a wonderful dinner, we listened to the Queen before enjoying Billy Smarts Circus, Disneytime, Cinderella a pantomime featuring Jimmy Tarbuck before Christmas Night with the Stars included Rolf Harris plus classic 'Til Death Do Us Part and Steptoe and Son.

Family life was great but unfortunately Grandma was not very well, she was now confined to her bed and I hated seeing her like this, every morning before we went to school we'd go across to spend time with her.

Grans legs had swelled so much that she could not walk very far, she was having her meals brought up to her and no longer was she enjoying the trips around the neighbourhood.

All the family rallied around her, it was now her time to be cared for after all she had done for the family in the past 35 years, she had raised and nurtured four children of her own, and all had done well for themselves.

William junior had married and settled in Grenoside, he had wed back in 1959 to a lovely lady, but at present they had got no children, I had only seen our Bill on a few family occasions, mind you it was a damn sight more than I had clapped eyes on his sister Jean, my ex-mother.

Bill's house was lovely. I only ever visited there on a couple of occasions, but I certainly could have lived in a house like that. He did attend the wedding of my mum and dad though.

Uncle Fred was the one I spent more time with, well he did live with us for a few years. He had built up his own construction company and I can remember going with him in his car to this development in a place called Everton, this I remember because it was on the morning of the cup final of 1966.

I can also remember my Granddad going around to see him after he had sacked my Uncle Mick for not shoring up this wall one Friday afternoon. When they arrived at work the following Monday the wall had come a tumbling down. He was livid and sacked him on the spot. Granddad was not happy because stubborn old Mick would not sign on, so was not contributing any money to the household.

He pleaded with Fred to set him back on. He told him to tell Mick to be back at work Monday morning.

Mick was only ten years my senior, and I liked him a lot, he was funny to be around, even though he had set half of my programmes on fire. He was so laid back he was horizontal, he was only 22, and living life to the full.

He liked his football even though it was the other lot he supported, he had plenty of mates that he hung around with, and would always be drinking in town.

Grandma had done a very good job with her children, and when they had moved into adult life, she started again with me and our Mark; she was back to square one, when she could have been taking it easy in her later
years.

She was back on her hands and knees, lighting that fire so the house would be warm before I got up to go to school. But I was nearly seven so could at least help dress myself but our Mark was just a baby, and needed round the clock attention, and this he got.

She was repeating exactly what she had done for me at that age, but this time there was no respite, or mother to hand him back to, when she was tired.

I can never really remember a time that she was not there for me and our Mark, and I hated seeing her like this as we passed through on our way to school.

I was now growing up fast and at the age of twelve, my mate Wesley had got us an invite to a party in Burngreave, and I was really looking forward to this. Some nice girls from school would be there, we played this game where all the boys and girls names were placed in separate piles, once two had been chosen you got five minutes at the bottom of the stairs to get down to some serious kissing.

I don't think alcohol featured in the proceedings but we really enjoyed ourselves; in fact I'd not realised I was over an hour late from the time dad said I'd have to be home. As we jumped off the bus I saw dad was stood on the corner of Musgrave Road; he didn't shout at all but just put his arm around my shoulder and this threw me.

Parked up Musgrave Road was an ambulance and it was parked in the very same position it had been on the 3rd of November 1955, but this time instead of bringing new life into the family it was taking it away.

You see while I'd been having the time of my life, Gran was fighting for her life and this was one battle she was losing and on this day in 1968 she sadly passed away.

Why had I gone to that bastard party? I should have been there for her like she had been there for me. I had tears in my eyes, mum had gone in search of Uncle Fred, he was at Auntie Dianne's parents in Darnall when he was finally located, he too had been enjoying himself just like me and he was playing cards when mum broke the sad news to him.

At least she had not died alone, Granddad was there as always by her side, they had too suffered there ups and downs but were still together after 35 years, finally that great lady could now take a well-earned rest, mind you I bet she would be giving him upstairs a piece of her mind if he ever stepped out of line.

I'd never got the chance to say goodbye and thank her for all she'd done, I was even missing when she was laid to rest in City Road Cemetery.

My schooling suffered for a short while, I would have a tear in my eye after I'd took a short cut across Gran's back garden, and turn to stare at the kitchen window in hope that she would be stood there.

I only had to survive a few more weeks before we broke up for the six weeks holiday, my first year in senior school had been ok, I'd managed to stay out of trouble unlike one of my close mates.

We had gone to cheer on the big lads who had got to the final of the football tournament, they were a very good team, and we had travelled in good numbers to show our support. It was at the Co-op ground on Bellhouse Road. I cannot remember what the score was at the time but one of the big lads thought it would be funny to throw an egg at the opposition goalkeeper, but he didn't have the bottle.

At first he tried to put it in my hand but I was not having it, then he turned to my mate, he was like a rabbit caught in the headlights and before he knew it he was fondling the egg, everyone was egging him on, but not me.

I was a goalkeeper and I would have hated it if that had happened to me, I cringed as he threw it and found its target. The match was immediately stopped and a thousand pairs of eyes homed in on the ragamuffin gang situated behind the goal.

We scattered in every direction, I was not getting collared for something I had not done, and headed home. The following morning every entrance to school was manned by a teacher, and I was dragged to one side. They knew I had not done it because my mate had been grassed up.

They just wanted me to confirm that he was the culprit. But I just told them that the egg came from behind me and I did not see who threw it, later on that morning my mate was hauled out of class.

After writing a letter of apology he received a few strokes of the cane, up to now I had endured the ruler and slipper but not the dreaded cane.

At dinner time he was showing off his battle scars that were on both hands, he had copped for the maximum that was three on each hand.

I bet that put him off eating eggs for the rest of his life. Another lesson learnt - do not let anyone bully you into something they are not prepared to do themselves, it was probably the bully who grassed him up in the end to save his own skin.

My mum hated life on the Shirecliffe. She would dread that bus travelling through the Wicker before passing underneath the Arches, it reminded her of her childhood visits to her father's side of the family on the Parsons Cross.

His sisters were blind and they felt it necessary to feel what Marie, Patricia and David was wearing. They hated these weekend visits and pleaded with their mother to put a stop to them. When she was younger she didn't mind it, kids just got on with it, but when she moved into her teens she made a stand and refused to go anymore.

This brought her at loggerheads with her father but her mother stood her corner and thankfully those weekly trips through those dreaded Arches came to an end. But they had now been rekindled with us living in Sheffield 5.

With the passing of my Grandma this prompted her to make the move. They had previously spoken about my mum's desire to leave the Shirecliffe. She had assured my Gran and Lily that where ever we ended up they would be more than welcome to visit. Dad on the other end was set in his ways and hated change, this led to endless bickering. Oh! I thought, here we go again. Did he never learn that you cannot win if the woman of the house wants her way?

One near neighbour told my mum that her brother Tony had been granted a golden key by the council because his home on Penistone Road was due to be demolished, at present he had a pigeon loft in his back yard, so needed them to be rehoused.

Most areas in the city were not flying rat friendly, houses on the Shirecliffe were hard to come by, probably due to that fact that these areas in the north of the city catered for the pigeon fanciers.

Mum met with Tony's wife and they made a visit to the council, she fancied a property on the Norfolk Park, these properties had a waiting list of nearly two years, they also looked at Intake but these too you had to wait well over eighteen months.

So much for these golden keys, how many had the council handed out? When everything looked lost, the girl at the council noticed that a re-let had become available on the Newstead Estate at Birley, but where was this mum thought?

The girl enquired with her manager and he showed mum a map of the area. It was further out than Intake and bordered on the estate of Frecheville, it used to be in Derbyshire but with the new boundary change it had moved within Sheffield's border.

Mum and Mrs Green headed for Pond Street, strike while the iron was hot was her motto. They caught the bus and alighted at the bottom of Birley Lane.

This lane separated the estate from the fields beyond, it looked idyllic, and Mrs Green was also taking a shine to the area, but she knew it was a non starter as far has she was concerned because, those pigeons were not allowed in this neck of the woods.

Mum automatically fell in love with the place; it was so clean and fresh, no lorries dumping the city's waste on your doorstep, and no lighting of fires every morning because these houses had gas central heating.

It was number 31 Newstead Rise that was on offer, the two intrepid explorers were noseying around the property, and then all of a sudden a workman opened the door. Mrs Green asked if they could have a look inside because they had been offered this house. The man said it was in a right state because the previous tenants had been evicted, he reluctantly let them in. He was not kidding; how could people live like this my mum thought? They had even pissed all down the walls and the stairs.

This did not put mum off, she wanted this place to call home, and made a beeline back to the council offices before they closed for the evening.

When dad returned home from work she told him that they had chance of a house on the Birley, but dad was set in his ways and enjoyed life on the Shirecliffe and change was not good.

Again mum let rip and told him that once he had finished work tomorrow he was to meet the rest of his family at her mother's on the Manor.

Dad reluctantly turned up and with Sam in tow, they made their way to view this house that was on offer. Why had he not listened to her in the first place because him and Sam were of the same opinion as my mum, the place looked great, and once they had returned and given their seal of approval mum would set the ball rolling the next day.

Everyone was now happy. Mr Green was busy re-assembling his pigeon loft in our back garden, all we were waiting for was the council to give us the green light, but before that we were embarking on our first family holiday, along with Auntie May and her three girls, Glynnis, Nicola and Tina, we were heading for Walsh's caravan park in Skegness.

We must have looked a right sight as we made our way towards the bus station, four adults and six kids, with all our worldly goods in one great big white suitcase. How long it took to reach our destination I will never know but I bet we had some laughs on the way.

Well we finally arrived in Skegness, and Walsh's Caravan Park was massive, it had row upon row of manky caravans, ours was so tiny I knew what sardines felt like when they were put into that tin.

David was only one year old, mum had managed to acquire credit so that the kids could have new clobber, I got myself a new pair of plimsolls and would be christening them this holiday.

We were playing ball with some kids from the other caravans and had got ourselves a nice game of football going, mind you I tried to bust the back of the net with one shot and my brand new plimsoll was orbital bound. Auntie May's daughters thought it would be funny to run off with it and I was not pleased at all.

They'd run off and took it into the ladies toilet block, I was having none of it and burst in just as one old dear was pulling her baggy knickers up. She aimed a good old slap to the back of my head but missed by inches.

Now it was getting beyond a joke and I honed in on my solitary shoe. Before I could get hold of it, the silly bitch threw it into a cubicle. Unfortunately for yours truly it fell down the gap between the breeze block wall. I was perched on this shithouse wall staring down at my very sad lonesome slipper, it was only about seven feet away but it might as well be on the bleeding moon because I could not hope to retrieve from there.

One bright spark suggested that we get one of those long poles that they use to open and close the windows at school, we were on a shitty caravan park in the middle of nowhere and he comes up with that idea.

I was none too pleased with the girls and they really deserved a slap. When I thought that all was lost and I had to go and explain how I'd come to lose my brand new footwear, a kindly lady appeared carrying a prop.

Who brings one of those on holiday I thought to myself?

It turned out that some of these caravans were privately owned and the occupants brought all the home comforts and they used the prop to hold up the weekly wash.

Bingo it took us all of five minutes to spear the offending footwear and have it firmly planted back on my foot, I'd just got back to the caravan in time for tea when the heavens opened and did it rain. It rained during the night and the whole of the next day and the day after that, and the day after that, we were confined to barracks; cards would be played, draughts would be played followed by snakes and ladders and ludo.

Mum had suffered from a throat infection, and the doctor was called, he prescribed some antibiotics but the chemist was in Skegness, dad had to walk all the way there and back because we didn't have the price of the bus fare.

He certainly was not using the little beer money he had on public transport, it took a couple of days for mum to make a full recovery, just in time to pack up all our worldly belongings and make the long journey home.

I could not wait to get home and play with my mates, too many women in such a confined space were not my idea of having a good time.

So after I'd finished my first year in senior school I was supposedly off to pastures new but I was not keen, like my dad I was happy on the Shirecliffe and loved my schooling. As it was the six weeks holiday I never got chance to say farewell to my school mates and was not a happy bunny.

At least Gran was not here to see us move, this would have probably broken her heart. She'd grown that close to my mum that she referred to her as her daughter in law even though this pissed off her side of the family, the Marriott's from Southey Green.

But times were a changing and it would do our family good to put the past behind us, my guardian angel had now gone so now was the time to move on.

The Move to Pastures New

It was the summer of 1968, the time of free love and peace and all that crap, one minute I'm on the top field with the gang re-living Manchester United's epic victory over Benfica in the European Cup Final and the next minute, I'm off to a place called Birley; it was that far away from Sheffield 5, it used to be in Derbyshire.

Well we finally got the go ahead to make the move, I was being transferred from Shirecliffe to Birley, no fee was ever discussed but some unlucky kid was going to be upset, having to sit out the forthcoming football season while I took his place in the school team.

The removal company finally arrived one Friday morning in July 1968 and packed all our worldly goods on-board and we were ready for the off on this new adventure.

We didn't have a deal to take because my parents were still paying off the tab my dearly departed Grandma had run up, we drove off and waved goodbye to number 23 Musgrave Road.

I then took one last look at Wesley's house on Longley Avenue West and remembered all the good times we'd shared; once we had passed through the town and headed up City Road to the Manor Top.

We were not far from my mum's parents' house on Queen Mary Crescent, down Mansfield Road and another cinema called the Rex at Intake.

I thought we were never going to get there, we then went past a massive row of shops at Frecheville and we were nearly home and dry.

We turned into Newstead Road and bloody hell, I thought to myself this Vic Hallam must be a right skanking bastard because he'd not put any roofs on these houses, they stood like soldiers to attention in their shabby grey uniform look.

Ours was number 31 Newstead Rise, situated right on the end of the estate, our kid was in a trance staring at the wild animals in the field opposite, mind you it was the first time either of us had seen a cow in the flesh, we must have moved to the countryside because everything looked so green and fresh.

I ran into the house and the living room was that big, you could have played football in it, boy was it massive. Then upstairs and into the great big back bedroom that overlooked a very tidy garden that was fenced off, that bedroom would have been allocated to mum and dad.

Another one at the back and that looked just right for me and our Mark, while baby David would be having the tiny front one all to himself.

How times had changed; only five of us to share this massive upstairs which also included a nice bathroom. No more getting bathed in a pot sink or tin bath, and having to spend a penny at the bottom of the garden like we did at 112 Hoyland Road in Neepsend.

Or sharing a room with your parents for seven years, like we did in Musgrave Road, and no more getting up in a morning to a freezing cold house before the fire was eventually lit to brighten up the mornings.

Back downstairs and into the kitchen, it had a nice sink and cupboards and a place for the cooker to be connected. I asked my dad why we had no fire in the living room, his reply was swift, not got one we now have central heating that runs on gas.

The house did look empty with our worldly belongings thrust in one corner.

Uncle Roy told us on our journey up to the house that we were paying for the removal by the hour, and once we had come to a stop all us kids were to carry anything we could handle, we were like a line of ants carrying all our worldly goods in unison. Our near neighbour, Mrs Batty who lived at number 43, must have thought, good god who is moving in now?

Well after we had helped the removal men finish unloading all our belongings in ten minutes flat, this was it, we'd landed on the other side of our fair city.

David was planted in the back garden while the rest of us helped put the boxes in the appropriate room, mum thought we were getting in the way, so we decided to scour the estate, mum gave us a couple of pound and a note for the man at the local chippie; we were told to bring back the dinner, and what a lovely smell drifted from the chip shop.

Mr Scrivens who ran the chip shop must have thought he was feeding the whole estate when we handed him mum's note, a quick visit to Mr Farrelly for some sweets for after our dinner and we were heading back home.

I'd never seen as many trees and greenery in my whole life, the estate was topped off with a wide open space bang in the middle, with signs stating that we were prohibited from playing ball games.

Are they joking? I'd never seen anything like it in my life, now miserable old Vic was certainly starting to piss me off.

The old lads would have set them on fire, but what about the kids of the estate? Why did they put up with it? But that question would have to be answered later, because the chips were getting cold.

It appeared that the electricity and gas had not been switched on and while we had gone to the shops, Auntie May rang the powers that be at the nearby works department and told them that we had a small child and waiting until Monday to get the electricity on was not acceptable.

We were all sat in our new home demolishing our chip dinner, when a man appeared at the door, he'd come from the local depot and immediately sorted out the gas and electric.

He told my mum that the public amenities departments would not be reading the meters until Monday, so we had free gas and electricity until then.

Auntie May immediately put the water heater on and one after the other she bathed her three kids, well waste not want not was the motto of the day, even her and Uncle Roy copped for a freebie.

Once we had all enjoyed a free soak we waved goodbye to our neighbours from Shirecliffe, and they left to make the incredible journey home.

Mum had worked out that this house would be ten shillings a week cheaper to heat than the one with the old coal fire.

How clean was this house? No more falling soot unlike the time just before Christmas 1967. Usually you had the local sweep round once a year to clean the chimney, but with money being hard to come by mum decided to do an old fashioned do it yourself job. So once she had packed us off to school she set about cleaning it.

You see if you light enough paper and send it up the chimney eventually it should catch fire and with a bit of luck send the unwanted soot cascading down the chimney. All the furniture had been covered and the carpets removed so she waited with the bucket of water just in case the soot was alight.

Everything went like clockwork, the soot fell, the water put out the flames, good old mum had played a blinder except for just one thing, she'd forgotten about our David laid in his pram by the side of the fire.

The poor bugger was covered in it, she grabbed him and ran upstairs to give him a good scrubbing, and he came up a treat, she must have had a right old panic on with our kid looking like he was auditioning for the Black and White Minstrels.

My mum and dad did get the honour of getting the master bedroom, while old sooty face got the front one, I also had my own single bed thanks to Uncle Fred and the days of sharing with our Mark were long gone.

They must have got on the top of things with old Mr Swycher because new things started appearing in the home like a brand new television set but still it was in black and white.

Grandma Flo had really taken my dad to the cleaners and had even forged his signature to cash in an insurance policy, this never tainted my memory of my guardian angel in later years and I thank her for everything she did for me and our Mark.

Our block on Newstead Rise was bursting with kids so they were loads of new friends to be made, but most were a lot younger than me but this suited our Mark.

Only Gary Lillyman from the house opposite was about my age, we soon became good friends and along with John Biggins and Terry Loukes they soon were showing me what life was like on our estate.

I had a few more weeks of the holiday to go before I would be attending Birley School, I also found out why the no ball games signs had not been destroyed, we used them as goalposts.

Kids from the top of the estate included Bryan Grayson, Stephen Webster, Robert Bradley and Gary Drury, the latter was better known as Sam and nobody called him by his real name which was strange.

Robert Emmett was also another who got christened with the Sam tag along with Gary Ashton from further up the estate, after all those years in Sheffield 5, this place was full to bursting with them, while over in Shirecliffe we had been Sam-Less for years.

Football was a great tool to make new friends, I'd be out early doors every morning and make for that big green square in the middle of the estate, and it was a magnet for all the local kids.

When we were not playing football we would head for Birley Woods or just run through the cornfields, there was also a derelict mine and these big concrete containers that had loads of frogs and newts swimming about in them; this was the first time ever I'd seen a frog.

It was like being in another world, no lorries dumping rubbish 24/7 on your doorstep, the local farmers orchard was a right temptation and resulted in myself, Terry and Bryan getting caught pinching his apples; we got a right telling off from him and he told us to ask in future, before ceremoniously kicking us up the arse as we went through the gate onto Birley Lane.

Further afield we had the village of Ridgeway that led down to Ford bottom and a stream to play in, I can remember enjoying myself around the Rivelin Valley some years previous but that place was a bit hazardous to get to for young kids on their bicycles.

This place on our doorstep though was so peaceful, and every day saw a new adventure, whether we were making dens or climbing trees in Birley Woods or larking about in the farmers' fields or the abandoned mine, life was great.

Time just flew by and I'd really landed on my feet with this new set up. It also helped our Mark because when we lived back on the Shirecliffe he always looked pasty and white, now all this fresh air was doing wonders for him.

With the school holidays coming ever more closely to an end, I was getting myself ready to face another challenge, with my third school In as many years, and at first I was not looking forward to it.

The very popular Rex cinema had Saturday morning matinees just like the Forum and Essoldo had done over at Sheffield 5; here though we would pay for a couple of us to enter the premises, and when the lights went down they would open the emergency exits.

Kids would come flooding in. We were quickly growing out of this early morning tradition, and our visits would diminish as the months went by.

Well the day had come and I was wearing my new maroon blazer that mum had got for me, my old black blazer that I'd worn so proudly on my first day at Shirecliffe Senior School had now been made redundant.

I walked up to school with my mum before she went to the junior school to fix our Mark up, I was shown to my form room to have the register taken, the teacher then gave me a jotter and a new pen, the rest of the day passed me by and I couldn't wait to have my trial for the football team.

Mum loved life on the Birley and even though our resources were stretched to the limit with dad only bringing home about £12 a week, times were hard, but enjoyable.

None more so than the Tuesday morning ritual to the Post Office to collect the weekly family allowance of nine shillings. She would push our David along Birley Moor Road to join the queue that stretched the length of the Frecheville shops.

With the meagre amount pocketed it was first call at the bakers to sort out the bread, then the butchers would be visited and the ingredients for the family stew would be purchased.

She would then treat herself to a freshly cooked pig's trotter and enjoy that while she returned home, occasionally breaking a tiny bit off to feed our kid.

When we returned home from school the house smelt so inviting, she'd spent all the day baking rows upon rows of jam and lemon tarts that lined the kitchen side.

Mind you I bet these plates had not seen a fish dinner, sorry Gran; the stew would be simmering on the cooker and the smell of freshly cooked Yorkshire puddings would fill the air, we would always have a freshly cooked meal every evening.

Friday teatime was so regimental though because this was knocking on the door night with visitor after visitor coming for literally their pound note of flesh.

Dad had returned from work and that little brown envelope would have been emptied onto the kitchen table and a pound note would have been carefully inserted into the cards that lined the kitchen side.

You see it was payback time. The Provident lady would be first in the queue, she would hand over £20 every Whitsuntide and Christmas and in return you'd give her back a pound a week.

Wigfalls where we got our electrical items from would do exactly the same, but the old man who was a regular visitor handed over cash and in return you paid him back an extra pound on what you borrowed.

Here we see our David attempting to blow out his very first candle in August 1968 surrounded by the neighbour's kids which included Marie and Alan Batty, Gary Lillyman and the Spooner brothers; our Mark is holding onto him while my cousins Helen and Julie get ready to give a helping hand in blowing out that solitary candle.

August was also the start of a brand new football season, unfortunately I was now a million miles away from Hillsborough, and I didn't have my Grandma or Uncle Frank to fund my football.

I scoured our forthcoming fixtures and the visit of the newly crowned European Champions Manchester United was to be played on the 31st of August. I asked my dad for the

money for the match, although money was in short supply I was hoping that he would back a few winners the previous Saturday and be rolling in bundles of cash.

Mind you if I relied on him winning on the horses to fund my football I'd never get to the match.

Anyway come the day of the game, Bryan and Terry were my new match day accomplices. It took us ages to get to the ground, and by the time we got in, my usual vantage point was full to bursting. We proceeded to push and shove our way to the front, it was a good job I was a tall, skinny bugger.

The weather was also fine with the sun was beating down on us; I felt a million dollars.

When the teams took to the field Manchester United had the likes of Charlton, Law and Best plus that funny looking Nobby Stiles who only two years previous was dancing a jig around the historic turf of Wembley clutching the Jules Rimet Trophy or as it was better known, the World Cup.

Wednesday opened the scoring to the delight of all around us, our joy was then short-lived with United scoring two quick goals before big John Ritchie levelled; again United went further in front with Bobby Charlton.

Denis Law and George Best in terrific form, just before half time Jack Whitham scored his second of the game.

What a first half we had just witnessed, I had seen some great games in this stadium like the time we beat Chelsea 6-1 and Burnley 7-0 in 1966-67 season.

The second half got even better when good old Nobby put through his own goal to level the scores at 4-4 before Jack Whitham hit what we didn't know at the time was the winning goal to hand the Owls a fantastic 5-4 victory, Jack was later credited with the own goal to bring his personal tally to four.

After the game was over we just walked and walked towards town along Penistone Road, were we on cloud nine or what, we had just turned over the European Champions.

Mind you the Owls brought us back to earth some four days later when we were dumped out of the League Cup by fourth division Exeter City.

With money again hard to come by, I didn't push too hard for my fortnightly football fix, I would pick my games and it was the visit of Liverpool in November that had me next heading for Hillsborough.

Even though I was only 12 at the time I knew that my mum dreaded that thank god it's Friday feeling.

I can remember Gran playing this game every Friday, she would grab both me and our Mark and we would play hide and seek. You see the three of us would hide behind the settee while the rent man would knock on the door. He would then knock on the front window while having a good nosey to see if there was any sign of life indoors.

Nine times out of ten he would return to the council rent department empty handed, minus the money that was owed on the property of number 20 Musgrave Road.

Our David would now be the one left at home while his two big brothers went about their education, mum would place him on a rug in the back garden when the weather was nice and set about her daily chore of keeping the family home nice and clean, she would busy herself in the knowledge that the youngest sibling would be safe and secure in our back garden.

Unfortunately Dad was not very good at the old do it yourself; time after time she had asked him to make sure that the little one would be contained for the period.

David would have other ideas though and would squeeze through the smallest gap in the fence and make a break for freedom, he didn't wander far, he just liked Mrs Simcox garden better, and many a day she would return him to my mum with a face like thunder, and the words of can you keep him from escaping again.

Birley school was great and we had some fine teachers, Mr Carpenter was the aptly named woodwork teacher, Mr Fiddler I think taught history, when he ever got around to it because he would go on and on about how good his beloved Sheffield United were, or as he put it the super Blades.

Mr Reid taught English and ran the physical education department; Mr Clarke did the old religious thingy while Mr Kirkwood was the master of music.

Miss Adams was the lovely French teacher, and boy was she lovely, with Mr Phipps giving his insight into all things science that just about completed the line-up.

Miss Baker ran the art class, she once tore into me for messing about with a load of lollipop sticks instead of getting on with my work, we were supposed to be doing a collage and if she had waited for my work to be completed instead of giving me a hard time, then she would have realised that my work of art was a park bench made out of lolly sticks that was connected to the background mural of kids playing in the park.

The following week my masterpiece was sitting proudly on the art room wall, that subject was my all-time favourite, and I wished we could have had that lesson every single day.

But it was not education that I was after for the time being, I needed to get into the football team, I'd always been number one during my Shirecliffe days apart from the time I was side-lined with my broken arm.

Mr Reid was now the person I had to impress; he looked after the sports side of things and was also a very good English teacher.

Someone had already informed him that this new kid was not a bad goalkeeper.

Birley under 13s held their trial in the first week of the term and the kid who held the jersey last term was Graham Brunt, he didn't look too happy as we started the game.

I loved every minute and was in commanding form, as we left the field Mr Reid told everyone that the team would be posted outside the gym on Thursday.

I could not wait for that day to come and knew from the off that the list would start with 1. Cronshaw, and boy did we have a good team.

We were entered into the Radley Cup and the teams were split into two groups with the top two qualifying for the semi-finals, we had avoided our local rivals Frecheville but we feared no one.

Our very first game we travelled back to my old stomping ground where we played Owler Lane in Concord Park.

We were getting changed and our opponents were taking the piss, before the boundary change Birley played their football in Derbyshire, bloody hell these bastards must live on a farm they scoffed.

Looking around the dressing room I knew I had made the right choice and reverted back to my favourite and best position because last year at Shirecliffe we were having a pre-season friendly against Sheffield Boys under 11s.

I think Vic Spencer had set this up for us; anyway we were a bit thin on numbers so I volunteered to play at centre forward, and Christopher played along with Wesley and John.

Glenn I think had left and gone to Chaucer School, I didn't do too badly because I scored a hat-trick and was very pleased with myself.

I played the remainder of the year at centre forward but I think we lost more than we won and got thrashed at Hurlfield by 12-2 in the cup.

I did score our two goals though, and on criticising our goalkeeper, one of their players said if you can do any better than you go in, so I took him at his word and when I moved up to the Birley I retired as a outfield player.

You ought to have seen our first opponents of the season after I'd been made totally redundant most of the game because I really lost count of how many goals we scored, sorry boys but Owler you took one hell of a beating.

Not one to miss a trick I left them with the words of come on lads we need to get home the cows want milking, after we'd milked the boys from Sheffield 5.

Football was great for this new boy and how it helped me integrate after our move, mind you winning all the time made it a lot easier.

All season we won game after game only to come unstuck at St John Fisher whose centre forward I tell no lie had a beard.

They muscled us out of the game, but Mr Reid was good at his job and knew that we needed an injection of new blood to strengthen our team.

We drew St John Fisher in the semi-final of the Radley Cup and even though they'd recently beaten us, the injection of a couple of new players ensured we played out of our skins and edged them out by a 2-1 score line.

Mick Tarren, after playing all season, missed out on our moment of glory because he'd unfortunately sliced a tendon on some broken glass that put him out of action for the foreseeable future.

We were hoping for a local derby against Frecheville but they lost to Crosspool, mind you our only other defeat was to Frecheville in a friendly so we didn't under estimate the lads from Crosspool.

On the day of the final we were just too good and ran out 4-2 winners to take the cup back to Birley just in time before the cows came home.

My old teacher Mr Watkins from Shirecliffe did the honours in presenting us with the cup, he told me it had not taken me long to find a bit of success since leaving his school.

The local paper even mentioned our moment of glory, with the headlines of Annerson Double Gives Birley Victory; those who contributed to my moment of greatness included Clive Bown, Kevin Boden, Mick Tarren, Malcolm Deardan, David Shirley, Alan Smith, Martin Batty, Lea Brookes, Nigel Annerson, Steven Mangle, Stephen Mincher, Gary Annerson and not forgetting the unlucky Graham Brunt.

Birley school was great. I carried on my interest in the theatre when I grabbed myself a part in the school play, mind you I still got myself into the odd spot of bother after I'd enjoyed a trip to the seaside and purchased a couple bags of itching powder.

I went on the rampage at dinner time and put the afternoon's schooling into disarray because most of the school were in the showers, Mr Lines gave me a right old telling off and I'd not got off to a very good start.

This put mischief on the back burner because I liked everything about this school, I was even chosen to play in goal for the staff against those leaving school at the end of the year; we had the usual sports day but running round a track was not my idea of fun. Mr Phipps decided that because I'd not volunteered for any event he'd do it for me, yes yours truly copped for the mile and pole vault. Now running a mile was just about bearable but putting yourself ten foot into the air and landing in six inches of sand was not for me so I was ill that day with a bout of what was called vertigo, the fear of heights.

The mile on the other hand saw me chasing Ken Newton a prolific runner; mind you he only lapped me once or was it twice.

But the finale to the school year was all the school sat in the gym while the school leavers put on the boxing gloves, can you imagine that today kids? Fighting with no head gear, it was all blood and thunder and one kid downed all comers and remained unbeaten, he left to a standing ovation and became the school hero.

Do Like To Be Beside the Seaside

Here we see Grandad Sam with his colleagues from the transport department, minus his cap I might add. This was another chance to enjoy a summer trip to the seaside because the buses always ran a kids trip to Cleethorpes. It was now 1969 and with the added bonus of dragging our Mark along, my mum waved us off from Pond Street. We both had a couple of shillings in our pocket, plus the money that the bus company would be throwing our way.

This was by far the best yet, and a lot more sophisticated and refined unlike those rampaging ones from the Pitsmoor Club. This one also treated all the ankle biters to a nice fish dinner before it was time to head home.

How neat and tidy we looked with our mustard knitted jumpers that Grandma Gertrude had lovingly created, it had been a great day at the seaside and for once I was not wearing a bloody bib.

I had purchased a plastic football with my money and we had enjoyed the day out; it had been the best ever. Everything was so perfect, the money, the crisps, lemonade and fruit the organisers had provided plus the little envelope with two shillings and sixpence inside, and those lovely fish and chips.

We were enjoying our very last kick about in the coach park, when my ball went under the coach. Like a flash I was under to retrieve the lost ball, our Mark then kindly informed me that I was covered in axle grease and I was likely to get my arse well and truly tanned.

It had been an accident and like an idiot I tried to wash it off in the toilets which made it ten times worse than it already was.

What an end to a perfect day, but how was I going to get out of this unscathed? For once I just blurted out the truth and my backside was fortunately saved from humiliation.

Anyway it didn't take super gran too long to knock me up a replacement, and normal service was soon restored, because we had the joy of another two trips to partake in from the Pitsmoor and Manor Clubs, and I steered well clear of the underneath of those bloody coaches.

I was now thirteen and I was gearing myself up for a family holiday at Pontins in Blackpool, apart from the odd day trip and a week in a grotty old caravan this was to be the best yet.

Mum had got talking to Auntie Pat and she had told her about their planned visit to the Lancashire coast. How you can afford a holiday like that she enquired.

Uncle John was an electrician at British Steel but even on his wages that were a damn sight more than ours, it was a struggle to bring up a family in these times.

Apparently good old Provident provided this voucher and for £40 you could enjoy a week at Pontins, you started paying £1 a week the previous January and if you kept up the payments on a regular basis, then two weeks before you were about to go on your holiday the lady who collected the money would hand over your voucher.

We were told to go to the barbers and have a nice little trim, we pushed our David along to the shops on Frecheville and within an hour we all looked really respectable for our holidays.

Provident had also come up trumps with our holiday clothes, and how smart we looked as we got ready that morning. Dad on the other hand only had one cardigan and not a shirt to his name. All those collars he proudly wore when dating my mum had seen better days and had long since been binned.

Saturday morning it was time to leave our house and head for Pond Street, dad was carrying that great white suitcase that contained all the families' finery.

Mum was pushing our David in his new pushchair that Grandma Gertrude had purchased because his old one looked rather shabby; well we don't want to bring shame on the Manor do we.

He was nearing his second birthday and he had grabbed a free holiday because of his age, our Mark had just turned nine years of age and I was hoping he would find his own friends on this holiday so I didn't have to look after him.

Pond Street was our destination to catch the Sheffield United Tours bus to Blackpool; meeting us at the bus station was Granddad Sam and Grandma Gertrude, it was a great adventure, and at the tender age of 13 I was going on an all-inclusive holiday where they fed you twice a day.

Granddad Sam as always looked rather dapper with his freshly starched shirt and collar, and cravat draped around his neck, while sporting a jet black blazer and cream coloured slacks; Grandma always looked elegant as well.

Auntie Pat and Uncle John were also travelling by coach with my cousins Julie and Helen, they were only four and six respectfully so would not be tagging along with me when I got to Pontins.

What a rickety old bus were we travelling on, the seats were like concrete and wasn't I glad I had my newly purchased Tec-Sac jeans to cushion the ride, while our Mark had his flimsy shorts on, I bet his arse was throbbing by the time we arrived some three to four hours later.

On our arrival mum handed over the Provident Cheque to the receptionist and she in return gave us the keys to our chalet, I was sharing with our Mark and mum and dad had our David to contend with.

Once inside our chalet it was soon clear that we had acquired the standard accommodation, we had no toilet or shower/bath but who cared, we were at the seaside and who needed washing?

This place was the business, and the list of facilities was endless as I scoured the brochure: Ballroom, Theatre, Regency Ballroom for the teenagers, TV lounge, Amusement Arcade, Hairdressers, Laundry Service and Souvenir shop.

Two cafeterias that catered for your breakfast and evening meal, mind you our David had to eat in the nursery because he was not quite old enough to enjoy holding onto a knife and fork.

This place made me chuckle, who would have time to wash their smalls with so much to cram in during our seven day stay, and what possessed anyone to sit in front of the goggle box while the rest of the camp were singing and dancing?

I once walked past the Hairdressers and there must have been a hundred women having a blue rinse or had their heads stuck inside a great big bee-hive, could they not have had a nice little trim like we did before they set off on this holiday of a lifetime?

I pointed out to my dad that they had a bookmaker on site, his reply was blunt and swift, keep it under your hat son, and don't tell you're mum. To tell you the truth, I don't think mum and dad had brought that much money because we didn't really have any.

I had now got myself a paper round at the newsagents on the top of Occupation Lane, and I did the Stars plus the Sunday papers. I was on six shillings a week but I rarely saved any, it would be spent on the football which was now back on the menu.

One day on the holiday the girls decided to visit Fleetwood Market and Gertrude enquired why Jim was wearing that same sweater, night after night, Granddad Sam had even lent my dad a cravat to cover his bare neck, because it's the only one he has got came her reply.

Gran immediately thrust £3 into my mum's hand to purchase him a new one, but don't tell your dad though she muttered, mum got dad a brand new blue sweater to wear for the rest of the holiday, thanks to her generous mother.

Three Bars and a lovely Chip Shop finished off the adult heaven. But what did us kids have lined up? It was more a case of what did we not have. There was indoor swimming pool, cycle hire if you could ever get booked on or afford it, Roller Skating, Putting (I wished I'd got Uncle Fred's golf clubs) Cricket, Tennis and Football.

I entered the Swimming Gala but once again my diving let me down and I finished just outside the medals.

We had a Sports Day but running was not my forte, and again no certificate was forthcoming, inside. I tried my luck at table tennis and I was progressing nicely towards the final, only one more victory and I'd at least got a nice little certificate.

The door to the sports hall swung open and it was my mum, she informed me that our David was playing in the nursery and the afternoon bingo session was about to get under way, so please keep an eye on our Mark would you.

I could not believe it, I was bloody enjoying myself and now I've got our young un under my feet.

He just got in the way and my expectations of pinning a winning certificate on my bedroom wall slowly bit the dust.

So that was me done. As I glanced at the weeks other chances of winning a prize it wasn't looking very hopeful, I was not very talented on the singing and dancing front, no fancy dress outfit was included in my meagre wardrobe, I was too old for the bonny baby and the wrong sex for Miss Pontins.

Snooker and Darts were for the beer swilling adults like my Granddad William, who was probably tucked up in the Kings Head on Commercial Street.

The evenings were great. I was allowed to join the adults in the Ballroom, it was just like Sunday Night at the London Palladium, all that singing and dancing. Our Mark was with the million other little ankle biters that littered the dance floor, while David was fast asleep in his top of the range push chair.

After the entertainment we were getting ready to enjoy the Mr Tarzan competition, could I not believe it when my dad and Uncle John headed for the stage.
I closed my eyes tightly and stuck my fingers in my ears as the pair of them pretended to be Johnny Weissmuller, the packed auditorium was going mental and the boys had done well.
Sorry dad but Uncle John was unbeatable, he swept all before him and grabbed first prize while dear old daddy finished third.

Wasn't I thankful for the old never-never, not only had it brought me to paradise; I was wearing the proceeds of the twice yearly cheque as well.
We had been placed into two teams on arrival which were named after a brand of cigarettes, with our team Capstan being blue and the other Consulate red.
We were now nearing the end of our holiday and no prizes had been acquired by our family, the weekly football match had caught my eye and even though I was only a kid I fancied my chances of getting into the Capstan team.

During our trial I was running rings around the chain smoking and beer guzzling adults, they were physically stronger than me, so I played out on the wing and once I received the ball my distribution was first rate, nothing fancy but I kept our team in possession.
With the trial over I thought I'd done enough to make the starting eleven on the forthcoming final on the Friday the last day of our holiday.
I'd gone and done it, but this time it read 11. Cronshaw was on the left wing, brilliant just keep out of the way of the 15 stone full back and I'd be ok!
The game was played every week and was sponsored by Watneys who also at the time sponsored a professional competition.
My only downside was the match kicked off at the same time as the afternoon bingo session so I only had our Mark cheering me on from the side-line.
But who cared, I'd done my bit in our side's 1-0 victory and was the proud owner of a Watneys Cup Winners Medal, it was one better than those losers from Bramall Lane did, they only made the semi-final before going out to the eventually winners Derby County.

Playing Politics with My Education

Bad news was just around the corner though because in their wisdom the Labour government of the day had decided to abolish the Grammar and Secondary Education and replace it with the Comprehensive system.

It was a bloke called Crosland who was Secretary of State for Education who set the ball rolling in 1965, they saw it has a crime that at the age of 11, pupils were being tested and those with a bit of the old grey matter managed to grab themselves a bit of the Grammar School hierarchy, while the rest of us were thrown together in the Secondary system, the name says it all we were second class.

Why was it frowned upon to feel sorry for all those who failed their 11plus examination. So what we didn't make the grade because we were just not good enough?

You would never put the crap players at football in the school team, so why should our learning system be any different; those children that were clever deserved their chance.

How embarrassing was it when the teacher decided to play football in our sports lesson and select two captains to select the players, once all the best players had been divided and separated, you were left with the rubbish footballers and last but not least the fattest kids were always last to be selected.

The sadistic games master could have wrote down the teams and had them organised while we were changing, but no we always went through this sad ritual every time we donned our football boots.

In 1970 the Conservatives swept to power and a lady called Margaret Thatcher ended the compulsion to convert but it was too late the damage had been done and by 1975 the 11plus was scrapped altogether.

The name Birley would be lost to be replaced by Thornbridge, this did not go down too well and as we moved into the summer break we did not know what was around the corner.

After enjoying my greatest ever holiday in my life and the ending of the summer holidays I saw myself getting ready to embark on this new Comprehensive ideal, and I was not at all happy when I got out of bed on that frightful Monday morning at the beginning of September 1969.

I walked through our estate on that Monday morning and boy was I feeling grey, those surroundings all around me looked so grey and dull, this went well with my feelings and grey sweater.

It was only twelve months previous that I'd dragged my mum to school sporting my maroon blazer adorned so proudly with my Birley school badge, I cannot really remember who was with me this time, but I was not looking forward to my first day in this new-fangled Comprehensive education.

Why change it, what was wrong with some kids going to the Grammar School, they had worked damned hard to pass the eleven plus to enjoy the delights of Thornbridge and Chaucer Grammar while those who had failed like yours truly had to settle for first Shirecliffe Secondary then Birley.

We were assembled in the big hall and were addressed by our new headmaster a Mr Snook; he told us this was a great new beginning and all the children would be treated equal, or words to that effect.

He had also given another rip roaring speech at the end of the previous term, when he told all the Grammar School pupils that they were to be the guiding light to all those less fortunate than themselves and they could and would lead all the Birley pupils onwards and upwards.

It was rumoured that old Snooky liked nothing better than dishing out a bit of the old corporal punishment and anyone having the misfortune to get a detention was named and shamed at the morning assembly.

After the introduction of this new form of liberal education the cane was left to gather dust and rarely saw the light of day after 1969 until it was finally abolished in 1987.

All the classes were pinned to a great big notice board, and I was looking for the one that had all the third year pupils names on, I started with three set one and none of those names looked familiar, onto the list for three set two and one or two of the old lads including my near neighbour David Shirley had made this list.

Now for three set three, the lowest form number and yes you have guessed it, full to bursting with the Birley refugees, now that boosted my confidence no end.

It was called Streaming when you endured every lesson with the same form, I was very good at art but still I was in the bottom class and felt put out that I'd been labelled in this way.

I knew that those in the top form had all enjoyed a Grammar School education for the past two years but now I was sharing their school and their playground and they probably resented it.

Only twelve months previous the schools were fighting on the fields that separated the inhabitants of both, every time it snowed we would head for school early to stock up on snowballs. You see the road that passed our playground led to Thornbridge School and those wearing that snotty green uniform or as we hatefully called them Green Bugs, they would be easy targets.

We also held the upper ground and on the first sign of the enemy they would be relentlessly bombarded, hundreds of snowballs would litter the sky and wave after wave would be heading their way.

One poor lad was completed obliterated and hospitalised, you see the snow had turned to ice, and it was just like throwing bricks, we did not seem to care because we were not getting hit.

At the following school assembly it was decreed that during bad snowy weather the bottom school playground would be out of bounds in the mornings and after school.

Groups of kids would congregate together, I knew no one who had been taught at the Grammar School over the past year, I was also a new kid to this area, I had enjoyed my junior schooling over in Sheffield 5, so had not been to any of the feeder schools that provided the pupils for Thornbridge Grammar, most kids stuck to their own, but me I'd chat to anyone.

John Schoefield introduced himself and he too was not very happy about the current situation, but he was telling the story from the other side of the fence.

John attended Basegreen Junior School and was one of those who passed that examination; his family was very proud of him, none more so than his father, you see he too had gained a scholarship to enjoy a Grammar School education but his father had other ideas and told him to forget about schooling lad, you need to work.

So there was no need to take up the offer of a higher education because once you had reached school leaving age, it was off to work.

John told me that the teachers here were good but very strict, they had been learning Latin last year, but he thought that had been scrubbed for another language in the form of German.

Some of the kids from Birley were struggling with English nether mind French and now German, he added that during one blistering hot day the teacher once allowed them to loosen their ties, but under no circumstances were they allowed to remove their blazers.

No talking was allowed when travelling to and from lessons, I was beginning to wonder if we had enjoyed an easy life over the past two years with our secondary education, but what would this be like would we adopt the Tom Brown approached of strict discipline or the more laid back liberal approach that was sneaking in.

He told of entering the form room and the housemaster a Mr Eleanor was going on about Floreat Busli, and the kids were banging the lids on their desks, and the immaculately dressed sixth formers in their black blazers were driving them to frenzy, it was all bloody Latin for the flourishing house of Busli.

The prefects made you swear allegiance to your house, you had to give your last drop of blood for the cause, what was it with the house names in this neck of the woods, Busli was a Norman Baron who sided with William the Conqueror, who rampaged across Britain while the house of Morcar was another so called warrior who fought by the side of Harold the King of England.

It was a wonder they didn't arm the kids with bows and arrows and have them recreate the battle of Hastings every lunch time; thank god I'd swerved my 11plus with being a bit on the thick side.

Who Furness and Pictou was, was anyone's guess; they brought up the schools rampaging gang of four, while the previous year at Birley, it was the Spartans, Athenians, Corinthians and Trojans that were feeding the appetite of the blood thirsty kids of Sheffield 12.

While over in the more sedate area of Shirecliffe, their houses represented the Commonwealth countries of Canada, New Zealand, Australia and South Africa, while in the juniors we had such greats as Nelson, Scott, Kingsley and Grenfell.

But now Shirecliffe had been lost forever and replaced by the mundane title of Herries, like Birley before it, the name had been erased for the time being, but would they ever return.

All kinds of information was heading my way, of what I had been missing over the previous two years, it was so regimental this Grammar School malarkey, the first year boys had to wear short trousers the whole year round.

Their introduction to the system was to be ceremoniously thrown down a great big grass bank, bloody hell and I thought the pushing of heads down toilets was kind of barbaric.

They had the added bonus though of ogling the girls who wore short green gym slips with white shirts and green ties, trousers for girls were forbidden.

The traditional school blazer even singled out the poor from the posh kids, if mummy and daddy had a healthy bank balance then Walsh's the Department store would be visited and the top of the range green blazer with its distinctive badge that read Credite in Luciem which was Latin for believe in the light.

While those from a poorer background who had worked damned hard to get to this standard had to settle for a much more inferior one from the good old Sheffield and Ecclesall Co-Op, so there was still a pecking order that the kids had to adhere to.

Even the surrounding area to the school had kids being labelled posh, the privately owned estates of Charnock and Gleadless with their semi and detached houses had the pupils divided on the playground from those who lived on the council estates of Birley, Basegreen and Hackenthorpe.

And to make matters more unbearable the school did not encourage football it preferred rugby, the traditional sport of the Grammar school hierarchy. I was beginning to thank my lucky stars that I had swerved this type of education.

The teachers wore gowns, and the discipline was strict, the headmaster had array of canes at his disposal and was not averse to dishing out the corporal punishment on a daily basis.

Fiona who was from the so called posh estate of Charnock told that as a very nervous 11 year old in 1967, she had to endure verbal abuse from the rough kids of Birley on her daily ritual of walking past the school in the morning.

Her best friend Judith was less fortunate, she lived in Hackenthorpe and not only had she to manoeuvre her way through her estate, she found herself standing out from the crowd as her bright green uniform, lit up the dank grey Newstead Estate on her way to Thornbridge Grammar.

After the day was finished Fiona preferred to risk the grassy bank on her way home, which was alright in the summer months, but one slip in the middle of winter would turn that immaculate uniform of green blazer, white shirt, green tie, green gingham dress and not forgetting those green knickers into a sludgy brown mess.

They also told me that they had to prance about in bare feet, when participating in a bit of the old gymnastics, but those lovely green knickers and green skirts saw the light of day when hockey and netball was forthcoming.

The sixth form at the Grammar School wore black blazers making them stand out from the crowd, and they were the equivalent of the bullying killer whales that roamed the playground at Shirecliffe during the same period but these Tom Browns threw you down a grassy bank instead of pushing your head down the bog.

These two schools, Thornbridge and Shirecliffe, were only seven miles apart, but when it came to the rigours of the educational system, the secondary one was that laid back it was nearly horizontal.

Now we were one big happy family and for the next two years of my life I was at the mercy of a watered down version of what it used to be like as a pupil of the now defunct Grammar School system.

Thornbridge Comprehensive, September 1969 - Top row: (5th from left) Peter Burke, (3rd from left) Andrew Blackadder and (left) Colin Jacobs; Second row (6th from left) Bryan Grayson

Back row: (8th from left) Garry Annerson, (6th from left) Gary Drury; Middle row (7th from left) Graham Brunt and (6th from left) John Ashforth

Back row (11th from left) David Shirley, (8th from left) Alan Hutchinson, (7th from left) the author, (4th from left) Mick Tarren and (2nd from left) Nigel Annerson; Middle row (10th from left) Philip Wood; Front row (7th from left) teacher Ron Reid

Back row (far right) Terry Loukes; Middle row (9th from left) Clive Bown.

What a difference the amalgamation made, where were the long flowing gowns that were so majestically worn by the teachers, where are those great green blazers that were worn by boy and girl?

Only a couple of boys can be seen sporting the old school motto, the great uniformed look had been lost forever; this was it the great new beginning that had everyone playing on a level playing field.

I was not even wearing a blazer this term, my parents just could not stretch the family budget to include one, but my grey sweater looked nice.

The bell had now sounded and the scallies from three set three were gearing themselves up to test this new system we now had in place.

Again I cannot recollect what my first ever lesson was in this brand new dawn of my country's educational system, I am not being stupid but what bright spark decreed that I should be in the lowest of the low class to finish off my last two years before I made my way in the grown up world.

I started to hate getting out of bed in a morning before heading to school, no more was I kicking a tennis ball about an hour before class like I did on that playground at Shirecliffe Junior School.

No more was I proudly wearing my maroon blazer at Birley School.

Mum knew something was wrong because I was leaving the house with fifteen minutes to spare before lessons started.

Mr Reid had been side-lined with Mr Evans being appointed head of Sports, we'd had our school trial for the football team and I'd impressed once again and was looking forward to our first game of the season.

I always looked forward to seeing my name opposite the number one on the team sheet, and now was no different, even if my schooling was going down the pan my football was my only salvation.

How wrong could I have been when surveying the team sheet? Where were the Birley Boys, only four had survived from that cup winning side of the previous year. I was not happy and I don't think my head was right, so I told Mr Evans to stuff his football team and from that day never offered myself forward to the school team ever again.

Mr Reid was none too pleased, but even his advice fell on deaf ears, anyway they were crap, and not a patch on our very successful team of the previous year.

Don't get me wrong there were some good footballers that attended the Grammar School which included the likes of Peter Burke, Ian Rixham and Douglas Fisher, the latter two would represent our school for Sheffield Boys, even Ian admitted that those in authority at the grammar and now the new found comprehensive didn't care too much for the game of football.

They would rather preferred us to take up the game of rugby. I once went with my good friend John Biggins to watch the school team play rugby, and got roped in to make the numbers up, we were playing at nearby Westfield.

They were all dressed in the appropriate attire while we had to play in football shirts. I don't think I ever touched the ball all the time I was on the field of play, we got totally trashed, we even lost one player who was sent off for grabbing an opponent by the

throat. Their teacher was none too pleased when the lad decked him as well.
That ended my enthusiasm for the game of rugby, or as I fondly call it the chasing of the egg.

Our class was not that gifted but we knew how to enjoy ourselves. Richard and Raymond Wallis were two twins but looked nothing like one another, Nigel Annerson was a good friend, Bryan Grayson, John Ashforth and Gary Drury from our estate, Phillip Wood who would be known as the brylcream kid because he used his father's hair gel to great effect and always had a comb in his top pocket.

Hutch was the tough nut and John was about seven foot tall, we loved our little bunch of misfits, and trouble with a capital T was just around the corner.

I was not the only kid in class without the blazer, one or two of the others had not bothered, but we were still in the minority but it didn't bother us, I liked the new grey jumper that mum had bought for me.

We also had an influx of new teachers who attracted our attention, now Miss Holland god bless her had a great introduction, because she had a habit of sitting by the windows on the cupboards instead of sitting at the head of the class.

One day we put Raymond in a cupboard and shut the door, he only lit up and started blowing smoke through the keyhole; the class were in stitches until the very stern Mr Mullen restored order.

Poor Miss Holland was once showing us a slideshow which contained some nice photographs of the Canadian scenery, but the weather was nice outside and one by one we sneaked behind the curtains and were off out the window to enjoy a nice spot of sunbathing, when the lights were put back on, half the class was bloody missing.

Mr Gifford who we fondly named Josh or odd socks, because he had a very strange habit of turning up to school, in brightly coloured socks of two different colours.

He was our English teacher and he was great, while reading Tarka the Otter we managed to plug the sink and left the tap running slightly before it overflowed and lapped around his desk.

He even showed an interest in our den we'd made in the woods and would show us the art of climbing trees in our dinner break.

He was a great teacher and it was fantastic to be involved in his lessons, he was not strict but would not let you step out of line, he made his classes interesting and let you participate in the reading of some of the stories and made you feel welcome.

John must have seen an almighty slump in discipline, the place was in uproar, these new teachers were just not up to scratch, we were like a pack of wolves homing in on our intended target, we showed no mercy, one sign of weakness and we were in for the kill.

Some teachers who were old school tried in vain to help these new college graduates but it was no good they had lost it from day one, and the onslaught was relentless.

Now our school dinners gave me an opportunity to add to my finances, they would sit you on tables that housed eight pupils, that would also include two first years that did all the fetching and carrying, now when the teacher collected them I just handed in six dinner tickets and kept two.

She never bothered to count them and just added them to the pile in her hand, bingo I thought, so I tried it over the following four days and when I left school on that Friday I had ten tickets to sell the first thing Monday morning.

I also had two customers who had the ten shillings ready and waiting, those first year pupils bought theirs off me instead of going to join the queue outside the office, there was no discount but they did get free sweets from our own personal tuck shop.

The shop in question was a Gola sports bag, you see in our spare time the lads would visit the local supermarkets, and confiscate anything that was lying around, others would call it shoplifting, but we were fully paid up members of the S.L.A, the sweet, liberation army; at break times the bag would be retrieved and goodies handed out, to pay was to fail was our motto, or juvenis furs as the Latins would say.

We would undercut the official snack bar and make ourselves a nice profit, the mark-up was incredible because our stock had cost nothing. The school cloakrooms were our meeting place and it was our own little private club, we would talk about everything and anybody, one topic of conversation came up over and over again though, had we noticed how the girls in class were getting rather large in the chest area, and that we'd love to get our hands around them on a cold winter's morning.

The dinner ticket racket worked for a few weeks until one of my regular customers left and was replaced by a mate of the other youngster; he was not very bright though because the stupid bastard put his name on the back of his ticket.

During an audit they found that his ticket was well past its sell by date, he was dragged before the headmaster and grassed me up, thankfully though he told them that I had only offered him the one ticket, and he had purchased the remainder from the office.

Again I was dragged in front of the headmaster and said I'd found it and sold it on, he reluctantly believed me, but I'd had a lucky escape, he could have easily informed the police, and I could have been in big trouble.

With dinners off the menu we opted to walk over Fox Lane and spend our dinner money in the White Heather chip shop, it was my very first introduction to curry sauce that was ladled over my chips and fishcake, this was one hundred times better, than cheese flan and frog spawn semolina, how the school's catering department had got away with serving up so much dross over the years was anyone's guess, but we fell for it, hook, line and sinker.

Sometimes though when money was tight and needed for the match at Hillsborough, we would liberate our dinner from the very helpful cooperative, and head for Bryan's to cook up our dinner.

Things were still tough at home and while Nigel and Gary was dressed to the nines in their Wrangler Cord Jackets and Levi Jeans with their nice shiny brogues I had the irresistible Tec-Sacs and Safety Shoes from Firth Browns.

The invitation to accompany them to the Top Rank Disco every Tuesday evening was rejected out of hand.

Back on the school front I only had one pair of suitable school trousers and they had to last me from Monday to Friday, now any normal kid in this situation would make sure he changed before going out but not me, I knew better and that muddy piece of grass on Newstead Avenue was my downfall many a time.

I'd not get changed and would wake the following morning to find them caked in dry mud, I had to take drastic action. I would lay them in the bath and wash away the dirt with the household flannel. Mind you they were piss wet through when I put them on. So off I would go to school with my steel toe capped school shoes, wringing wet trousers and grey jumper, by morning break the mud would start to dry again and turn my trousers a kind of muddy grey.

I'd be excused to go to the toilet and with the help of plenty of bog roll I'd give them trousers another good soaking.

Did I ever learn to change before going out to play after I'd had my tea? Did I ever, and this ritual was sometimes reinacted on a daily basis.

One morning before leaving for school I could not find my school sweater anywhere, so I just plunged my hand into my wardrobe and pulled out this bright red jumper, off I rushed and just made registration.

We now moved through to the morning assembly and waited to sing our hearts out, you see when we sang the hymns the last word of every line would be shouted out with great gusto and this really pissed the teachers off.

When it was time to be seated Big John would move one seat to his right, this would leave one unfortunate kid without a seat, the rest of us moved up in unison, the soft lads chair was now situated at the other end of a very long row of chairs and he would have to walk all the way round to be eventually seated.

We found this rather amusing and reinacted this stunt every morning and boy did this also piss off our teachers.

On leaving the assembly I was pulled up by one teacher who wanted to know where my school blazer was, I told him in no uncertain terms that I did not have one because my special maroon Birley one was no longer acceptable. He viciously told me that I looked like a bloody fire engine at a funeral with my brightly coloured red jumper.

I thanked him for his concern and took his sound advice on board that it did stand out in the midst of all this black and grey, so I told him that when I got home I would seek out my school grey sweater and cut it to pieces and make sure my mum had this one nicely washed and ironed for assembly on Monday morning.

I never really had spending money as such, I tried to make my own money, my paper round was a godsend but disaster was just around the corner. Our Mark had badgered me for ages to help me and mum said it would do him the world of good.

So Sunday morning off we go to the paper shop, I give him all the houses on Thornbridge Road, he only had six papers to deliver, why did I not give him my paper bag?

Apparently he put the papers down and while he was delivering the first one, the wind caught the rest and had them strewn the length of the road, he panicked and headed for home.

With the job completed I looked forward to my breakfast, while I was tucking into mum's traditional English, the paper shop owner was knocking on the door, he had half a dozen disgruntled customers complaining that they had not had their papers.

He was not happy with me and sacked me there and then, rather harsh I thought, thanks brother that was all I needed, my only steady income was taken away from me.

Mind you probably it was pay back after the time me and Nigel had organised a wage dispute with the paper shop owner, he relented and increased our wages from six to eight shillings a week.

Back at this so called school, my education was sinking fast, I'd lost all interest, even art and physical education was taking a dive.

With my paper round gone, I went back to shoplifting to fund my activities; Hillsborough was again out of bounds and my visits were very rare indeed, I was treading a fine line with my visits to the local Cooperative and the inevitable happened and I got my collar felt. The shop manager read the riot act but again I managed to blag my way out of it, again the police were not informed.

A couple of days later on returning from school mum's face was like thunder, she'd been in the Co-op and the manager - who she had known from school - told her about my incident and was not taking further action.

Again I'd had a lucky escape and even when I blamed losing my paper round, that fell on deaf ears. I knew deep down what I was doing was wrong, mum never did tell dad and I repaid that by never stealing again.

Our David nearly got mum into trouble though, they had opened a new supermarket on Frecheville shops, it was one of these self-service ones, you were given a basket on entering the shop and you just put your groceries in the basket.

She was merrily pushing our David around the store and her shopping bag was hanging off the pram, once this was complete the lady on the till was ringing in the prices and mum was transferring them to her shopping bag, job done, just two more calls to make at the butchers and bakers and she was off home.

On arriving home dad was in the house because he was on twelve hour nights, he immediately put the kettle on, then helped put the shopping away while mum sorted out our David.

We had a big yellow kitchen cabinet that stood proudly on the back wall, this would store all the fresh produce and bread, we didn't have a refrigerator, so the perishable items were kept well clear of the central heating.

Once he had placed everything away including the tinned stuff that went into the cupboard near the sink, he shouted my mum; we have been a bit frivolous haven't we, now we normally only purchased Stork margarine, but dad had retrieved four blocks of best Lurpack butter from the depths of her bag.

Apparently young baby David had reached down and picked them up while mum had been busy doing her shop, she was mortified, and returned them to the shop without a moment to spare, well we had got used to the taste of crappy maggi-anne the local name for margarine, the best butter would have only upset our stomachs.

I was good at finding ways to ease the burden on the families slim resources, I hated asking for anything, I'd have loved to have the latest fashion, but they were even out of the reach of our twice yearly Provident cheque.

Mum was busy ironing and there was a knock on the door, it was this bloke from the council saying that we were a month behind with our rent.

Now I know money was tight but my parents paid the rent without fail; my mum's crime was that when she received her family allowance she paid four weeks rent, unfortunately she always did it at the end of the month thus we were always four weeks behind.

He wanted payment immediately and was a little bit stroppy with his attitude. I don't know what the figure was but it was well out of our reach, everything we had was on the tick and spare cash in some bank account was not on the agenda.

He was getting really high and mighty and lectured my mum on the actions that he could take if the rent was not forthcoming.

That was it, she was not having him coming into her home and threatening her, she told him straight, we have three children in this house and what do you think will happen to them if you threaten to evict us?

You at the council will have to look after them if you make me and Jim homeless, I have not got the money to settle the arrears, so you take my three kids and then you can throw me and Jim onto the street.

I'd managed to avoid the clutches of Banardo's and the Catholic Church, and now I was being offered up to the council rent man, well I hope he lived locally because I was not moving school again.

I needn't have worried because he was sent packing empty handed and again mum had won the day, she never lost a battle and fought like a tiger to make sure we had a settled home life.

Mum and Shirley had a visit from this bloke flogging cigarette machines, these little wooden ciggie holders held ten packets and they were priced at two shillings each, the following week he would call to re-stock them and collect the twenty shillings.

Well that was easier said than done because with the help of a screwdriver they could have the back off it by Thursday if they were short of the two bob they needed for their nicotine fix.

I loved watching him empty the box and pile the money up and say the immortal words, Marie your four bob short, she'd reply bloody hell Shirley the kids must have been into the box.

My mum and Shirley were a right double act and when the tally men came around every Friday for their pound of flesh, one or the other would be on the missing list and one or two of them would leave empty handed.

I used to watch as she put the money on each of the payment cards and worked out to the last penny what she would have over until my dad got paid the following Friday.

Here we are pictured just before Christmas 1969, I am wearing my treasured mustard coloured sweater, our Mark is now aged 9 and our David is 2.

Mum is holding our beloved poodle called Pepe, that little dog had me chasing the length of City Road in hot pursuit.

You see I was sent to the dog parlour on City Road, I was just about to enter the shop when our dog had other ideas; off she shot in the direction of town. I was finding difficult to keep up with the damn thing, off down Duke Street and the busy main road that separated the Park Hill flats and the now demolished Rag and Tag Market.

As she ran across the waste land a man grabbed her and she bit him, oh my god what was he going to do? I needn't have worried he said that it was only a scratch, I dragged that dog into Pond Street and made the journey home.

Mum took one look at her scruffy looking dog, she was dismayed that the state she was in before showing me the door to return to the parlour to finish the job. On that run to town I'd have given good old Ken Newton, our prolific runner, a right run for his money.

Then one Saturday while watching my dad pick his selections for his ITV Seven, it had me thinking, race after race I was glued to the television.

Again my dad had backed more losers than winners, and the bookie had once again helped himself to my dad's shillings until the same time next week.

Now I didn't have the money to set up my own bookmaking firm, but I knew where I could find a few eager punters.

At school the following week I asked Mr Becket if I could make a board game, and with his help I cut out a rectangle piece of timber. I then used a scribe to shape out a track, they were then divided into sections with each having an individual number. I left a few blank and stained them green, they were my fences; land on them and your horse was out.

Another two coats of varnish and my masterpiece was complete, Mr Becket loved it and so did I. Mind you he would have preferred it if I'd have made a chess board.

Word was spreading that I was holding a race meeting every break time and dinner, I thought that if I could get six having a go and pay out on five, I'd clean up a shilling a race. Twenty races a week and I'd have a pound in profit.

Each punter had to bring their own marker, my mate Bryan used the car out of the monopoly game, others would use the boot, hat and ship, and anything would do.

I also told Bryan that it would be better than visiting the bookies on Birley Moor Road to place his wager, he loved having a bet and would study the racing papers during lessons, but I preferred acting as the bookmaker I found it more profitable.

I could not believe it, the common room was rammed and shillings were heading my way, the first ever race was great entertainment, and I paid out eight shillings to the winner and kept two for myself.

I'd gone and done it, and this little piece of timber was a goldmine, and my trips to Hillsborough were back on the menu.

Every break I had eager punters wanting a share of the action, Christmas came and went and life was great, but like all good things they come to an end.

One punter was down on his look, and pawned his pen set he'd got for Xmas, his mother enquired why he was doing his homework with a scabby biro, and he blurted out that he'd lost it at school, not only had he lost it but lost it gambling.

It was a gift from his grandmother and his mother was none too pleased that he was one step away from gamblers' anonymous, he had not eaten at school for months and his every spare penny was heading in my direction.

Shock horror after Monday's assembly I got the call from Mr Russon to report to his office, there to greet me was my so called mate, his mother and our lovely headmaster. I'd been rumbled and before I could say Grand National I was on my way to the woodwork room clutching my pride and joy, for its appointment with Mr Beckett's band saw, tears were welling in my eyes, not that I thought that I'd done anything wrong but that I'd been caught.

Not long after that something happened to Mr Beckett's shiny red brogues, he used to take his shoes off and place them under his desk then swiftly change into his old woodworking shoes, once the school bell had sounded we hurriedly left his company, we watched through the windows has he tried to put on his lovely shoes, trouble is he was having difficulty removing the six inch nails.

Our little gang was now moving on in years, I had just celebrated my fourteenth birthday, and we were just hanging around the estate of the evening.

We would congregate around the phone box on Thornbridge Drive, if you placed a small coin in the slot followed by a sharpened lollipop stick, you could listen for ages to the latest offering that was being served up by British Telecom's dial a disc service, the Archies and Sugar Sugar reached number one and proved very popular.

The good people at the phone company changed the record every evening and how we spent many a happy hour huddled in that phone box.

One Thursday evening though we saw Richard and Raymond Wallis heading towards us and they were dressed smartly in soldiers uniform, apparently they had joined the territorial army at the Manor Top and after going for so long dressed in civilian clothing they had earned the right to wear the Queens uniform.

I, Bryan and Gary tagged along with them and thought let's put a bit of discipline into our young lives, we enjoyed that first evening at the barracks and dad was well pleased when I took home the papers for him to sign.

I was going to be a little army cadet, every Thursday, we would head for the territorials, a bit of marching and square bashing is all we did, mind you the bloke taking us didn't half like the sound of his own voice, and it was bleeding loud.

Dad had even forked out on a pair of army boots for me, and he loved putting a right good shine on them, I think it brought back memories for him, when he did his National Service.

The weeks and months passed by, and I was still enjoying this army way of life, if only for one day a week, but there were other things to keep us occupied the rest of the time, none more so than the football and my Owls were not doing too well I can assure you.

As we moved into January 1970 not only was my education sinking faster than the Titanic, but my football team Sheffield Wednesday were having a torrid time in the English First Division, those sad acts from across the city, Sheffield United, had got themselves relegated in 1968 and this brought great delight to me.

It was also the time of another tradition that can only be associated with this fine country, it was the third round of the F A Cup. I had seen some great matches over the years in this competition, either at Hillsborough or Bramall Lane, drawing with the mighty Leeds United before winning the replay at Elland Road in 1969, and who could forget that home game at Hillsborough in 1967, when Ron Springett played for the Owls in goal, while brother Peter played in the same position for Queens Park Rangers when Wednesday won 3-0?

At the end of the season both brothers swopped clubs with Ron returning to London while Peter headed north.

This time though West Bromwich Albion were the visitors to Hillsborough while over the other side of the city, United had drawn Everton at home. Most of the kids at school usually went to the Hillsborough one week and Bramall Lane the next, we were only kids and the increase of football violence ensured few going to away games.

That was left to the bovver boys that represented both clubs, we were torn this day though, was I going to watch my team play the unfashionable West Bromwich, or see United entertain Everton, I went to Hillsborough to cheer the Owls on to a 2-1 victory while over at the Lane, United were doing the same by the same score line, the following Monday at school we were glued to the radio because it was the draw for the next round.

We were huddled around this old transistor radio in the toilets, and listened intently as the Owls got drawn at home to Scunthorpe while the Blades got a glamour tie at Derby County, those who supported United were over the moon, and some said they would go to Derby. Andy my classmate asked if I fancied it, but I was not sure about travelling away and the risk of getting my head kicked in.

I didn't even support the Blades but he went on and on until one night after school we booked on with the Sheffield United Tours, who incidentally had nothing to do with the football club.

I think it was about uniting the good folk of Sheffield.

We booked inside that big green shed in Pond Street bus station, I didn't bother telling my dad because Wednesday were playing anyway so he would have thought I'd gone to Hillsborough, there were four of us from school making our way into the town that Saturday morning.

I had purchased the Shoot football magazine that had a free FA Cup wall chart inside, I cannot really remember much about the pre-match activities or United losing 3-0, it was after when we were trying to return to the coaches that the action started, there was running battles everywhere.

Andy was busy stuffing his red and white scarf inside his coat; it was frightening, massive big skinheads from both sides knocking lumps out of one another.

In the confusion we found ourselves in enemy territory, and well and truly stuck behind enemy lines, the Derby fans were throwing bricks at the long line of coaches that filled the nearby streets.

We eventually pushed our way to the front of the Derby mob and made a dash for the coaches, how we located ours I will never know, but thanks to this big Shoreham Boot Boy who dragged us on board before we were well and truly battered.

The police eventually drove back the home supporters so we could go home, I was now safe and proceeded to open my magazine and have a look at my prized wall chart, just as that great big skinhead was taking his seat.

The bastard ripped it out of my hands and tore it up, tha won't be needing that now after we have been thumped 3-0 will you. If I'd have been a bit older I would have battered him, but never mind I was hoping the shop had some left when I get home.

The season went downhill for me after that Wednesday had also lost to Scunthorpe and my team was heading for the First Division trap door.

I had watched them sink to the lower reaches of the table and now the crunch had come, but would we survive as we moved into the last week of the football season.

The day had finally arrived now, and after securing a point at Old Trafford the previous Saturday when the Owls drew 2-2 with Manchester United, we only had to beat Manchester City to avoid the despair of relegation.

All the lads met on our estate and we made our way to the top of Occupation Lane to catch the bus into Pond Street. Even though the month was April it was pissing it down with rain. We alighted at the bus station and headed for the soccer specials that lined Flat Street, still the rain was relentless as we made our way to Hillsborough.

We entered the ground at the Leppings Lane end and stood in the wedge that separated the North and West stands, at 7.30pm the match got under way and the Wednesday faithful got behind our team. It looked from the off that City wanted us to win because they even missed a penalty and took their star player Mike Summerbee off. He was replaced by a young lad called Bowyer and I don't think this bastard had read the script because he tore us apart and scored two goals to our one. As the final whistle blew I could not tell which were the rain drops and which were the tears that were rolling down my face.

This place had brought some great memories to me over the past seven years, now it was hurting to see all those supporters so upset in the knowledge that we would be joining our city rivals the following season.

I just wanted to go home, I just wanted to sprint up Herries Road and throw myself in front of Grandma's roaring fire, I wanted her to dry my tears and give me a good cuddle like she always did, but she was no longer there.

I was sat on the crammed soccer bleeding special as it crawled through the traffic into town, then through that litter-filled bus station to carry on this relentless journey home.

One thing was for sure, I didn't fancy school in the morning, I was totally soaked to the skin when I finally arrived home. There was no roaring fire to throw myself in front of, just that bloody central heating purring away.

So there was no hanging about. In no time I was changed into my pyjamas before enjoying a nice cup of tea and toast from the cooker's grill; how I missed that crusty bread that would be toasted golden brown in front of that fire, I still miss that to this day.

School was now turning into a nightmare, I hated every minute of every single day and I was missing more and more lessons. How could this be, from the age of four I had loved attending my various schools, now I couldn't give a damn.

We even devised our own private homework club, you see a couple of very smart minded kids put their now defunct grammar school education to a very good use. Once the bell had sounded for the end of the school day they would collect our homework and beaver away all night for the price of a school dinner.

These boys were the business and the answers to a test or small essay would be handed out. Kids would then sit on the bog transferring the results into their very own exercise book, before depositing the incriminating evidence down the pan, a couple of flushes and it was gone forever.

How smug were our faces when we handed in the homework that we had toiled over the previous evening; there was no time for playing out when it was bloody homework night, we were chained to that exercise book until the morning came.

We were still enjoying our Thursday night visit to the Territorial Army at the Manor Top, and this was to be a special night because we were going to be kitted out with a uniform to wear.

I received a shirt, tie, tunic and trousers, plus these leather ankle bracelets that were worn over your trousers and boots, this outfit was topped off with a beret, and I was now a proper little soldier.

The following week dad helped me get ready and how I looked the part as I stood to attention in our kitchen, dad had got out his old army photos to compare us and the resemblance was quite scary.

I marched off to meet my mates and how smart did we all look? On entering the drill hall we were met by some proper soldiers that did this for a living, they probably knew that in twelve months' time we would be leaving school and embarking on a career in whatever profession took our fancy.

Well they were striking while the iron or gun was hot, they had invited us to their barracks near York, and we would enjoy a weekend away from home, and sample the life as a soldier.

We were given a list of things to take with us. All the cutlery and dinner ware had to be made out of metal, the kind of things you get from the camping store. I purchased a mug for my drink but did you see the price of those tins or plates to eat your food off? I thought bugger that I'll take one of mum's best dinner plates.

Well the weekend was soon upon us and we met that Friday evening straight after school. They had provided a kit bag and everything that was on the list was neatly placed inside, our coach journey was great and we were dressed to literally kill.

On our arrival in York we were first shown to our billet to unpack, everything had to be neatly laid out on your bed; my civilian wear, knives, forks, spoons, mug, towels and toiletries plus my mum's best plate.

We stood to attention as we were being inspected, good old army fashion. He walked slowly up and down the line, and I will tell you the truth this fourteen year old was shitting himself.

He suddenly stopped at my bed and stared intently at my mum's best china, he grabbed it and dropped it on the floor, it was in pieces. The bastard yelled that is not unbreakable is it.

First lesson of army life, obey orders even when written down on a piece of paper, I only just survived this incident as we moved onto the camp cafeteria.

Luckily for me Bryan had a spare tin to put my food into, that's mates for you. He was even missing out on his pudding just so I could be fed, after our meal we walked out into the evening sunshine and planned to change into our civvies, the camp had its own cinema and social area where you could entertain yourselves.

As we were walking by this large, whitewashed building the door flung open and this soldier shouted at us. Come here he shouted, and pointed to me. What have I done now I thought? My other two so called mates disappeared sharpish.

He told me to remove my tunic, roll up my sleeves and put on this apron. I have never seen as many plates and dishes, pots and pans in all my life and they all needed washing. I did not like this one bit. The quicker I got through them the quicker I would be out of this place, but as soon as I got on top of things more would appear.

I was in this kitchen for hours and was piss wet through when I finally emerged into the now darkened base. My mates had enjoyed a free showing of the film M.A.S.H. I was too bloody knackered to sleep, the following day, we marched and we marched, we ran and we ran some more, we marched again, then ran a bit more, this was really taking the piss now.

I slumped on my bed, and tore off this bloody uniform, I must have spent an age in the shower. I changed into my civilian clothing and again borrowed Bryan's tin can, this time after enjoying some well-earned food, I made sure we steered well clear of that kitchen. My friends didn't fancy the pictures so we just enjoyed the recreational area and played snooker and table tennis.

The evening was over before we knew it and it was time for lights out. Our night's sleep was interrupted by the older lads giving our billet a visit and turning our beds over and giving us a good kicking, they scattered all our toiletries all over and made a right mess. In the morning when we were awoken by that horrible soldier who did my mum's plate in, he made us clean up the room before we could have any breakfast.

The weekend was finally over as we boarded that coach for the return journey.

As the bus drove through those gates back into civvy street, I put up two great big fingers to life in the army. I could not wait for the following Thursday to return the uniform to the Territorial Army.

I much preferred hanging around that telephone box anyway, listening to good old dial a disc.

I had enjoyed the walking during my weekend stay with the army, but it was the discipline that had me running for the hills. Sometimes we would plan to catch the bus to Castleton and enjoy the great outdoors, on one such visit we had found a great deserted cave, we would use it if the weather turned nasty, we would bring along tinder to make a fire, and firelighters to get it going, sometimes we were so disappointed when it didn't rain.

I can remember one particular Sunday when the heaven's opened and we got caught out, we made for our home from home, and were soaked to the skin when we got there, our jars were full of newts and I think we were wetter than those little creatures.

Gary got a nice fire going and i reached into my bag and pulled out a tin of soup, tins were appearing from everywhere, and in no time they would be piping hot thanks to the roaring fire.

I asked for the tin opener to put some holes in my tin, well I didn't want it exploding. What a bunch of intrepid explorers we were, not one of us had thought to bring something to open the tins with. We resorted to hitting them with bricks but it was useless, not one of us had brought a knife either, we never did get to enjoy that soup but we did get the newts home in one piece though and they looked great in that fish tank at the bottom of the garden.

We were now drawing a close on this new chapter on the country's educational system, and to tell you the truth I hated it, I hated being labelled third rate; I was good at art and woodwork but never got to show my true potential because we were forever pissing about in class. You would be trying to create something special, then the next minute a great blob of paint would appear from nowhere and land slap bang in the middle of the paper that you'd toiled over for the past bloody hour.

Retaliation was the key word and the art teacher would run screaming for the hills; she'd return with the hostile Mr Mullen, normality would be resumed for a short while but the man was fighting a losing battle.

Only twelve months previous all the teachers in this school were tyrants with a capital T and a visit to old Snooky for forty lashes would follow. But now the Birley lunatics had taken over this educational asylum, and we were in complete control.

They had totally fucked up my life, what had happened to that snotty nosed kid who dipped his beaker in the water and slapped paint onto the paper in Shirecliffe Nursery and Infants; the time spent with my head in reading books, and playing football and receiving a full year's free swimming at Shirecliffe Juniors, and nearly drowning myself trying to get that much sought after lifesaving certificate.

Dressed to the nines on my first day at Shirecliffe Senior School, joining in with the school drama society and getting a role of one of the three wise men dressed in mum's blue quilted dressing gown, then transferring to Birley Secondary, and that famous maroon blazer, pursuing my love of football and winning the Radley Cup, and enjoying those drama and art lessons, school had been such a happy place over the past few years, now it had all disappeared down the pan. I was determined to go out in a blaze of glory when we returned for the very last time in September 1970.

Victor (No Ball Games) Hallam

Vic Hallam operated his factory in Langley Mill where he constructed prefabricated buildings, these he located at the Derbyshire Miners Holiday Camp in Skegness, and other resorts around the country.

It was after the war that he got involved in constructing school buildings due to the distinct shortage of classrooms, the then Derbyshire Council had three schools constructed at sites in Frecheville, Hackenthorpe and the record breaking construction of Birley Infants School that was completed in only 104 days.

He then turned his attention to providing nice clean affordable housing and constructed sites at Norfolk Park, while undertaking a larger project in the South of Sheffield, where he constructed the estates of Scowerdan, Weaklands and Newstead; these were collectively known as the SWAN estate.

They were a childrens' paradise, gardens with fences that were just right for jumping, greenery everywhere, wide open spaces for any and every ball game imaginable.

He had done good in this respect, and the kids thanked him for it by totally disobeying those stupid signs that littered the estate, the local ankle biters just wanted to have fun, and his well-planned lay out was just our cup of tea.

We liked to play football on Newstead Avenue, my school friends would complain sometimes when I had forgotten to change my footwear. I would still be playing in my school shoes and Terry and Stephen would insist that I either went to change them or play in goal. The Avenue though was not our favourite place to play football, this honour was bestowed on that small piece of land next to the garages on Newstead Rise. Old Vic Hallam had put a lot of thought into planning the lay out of the estate, the paths between the houses were great for racing your trollies or box carts, and we would also use them when having running races, just like the Olympic Games.

The kids of the estate would love competing for the gold, silver and bronze medals, there would be sprints, middle and long distance races, we even had a steeplechase where two kitchen chairs, a broom and our David's old plastic bath filled with water would be used. The shot-put was half of a house brick, the javelin was a sweeping brush, I don't think we used the discus just in case any windows got smashed.

I was always well out of the medals, Terry was the best runner and his chosen country was always head of the medals table, the final event in the Newstead Olympics was the marathon, the ages of the kids taking part ranged from fourteen down to nine.

I know the young ones never won anything but they just liked to join in, looking back this would not be allowed in today's climate of health and safety.

You would have about fifteen to twenty kids lined up across the length of Newstead Road, all wanting that gold medal.

I was not a bad runner, but not in the same league as Terry, Gary or Stephen; once we had got the starting signal that was it, I treated it like a sprint, I knew that if I was to be first to reach the Elm Tree public house at the Manor Top I would have to get a good lead.

I had left them trailing well behind as I passed the shops at Frecheville and then made that descent towards Intake.

Now the hill started to climb, and climb and climb some more, I was struggling and dared not look behind me, I was still in the lead though as I passed the Woodthorpe pub, but I had been done in.

I could see the Manor Top, but where were the rest? Just behind me was the answer, one by one they went past, I was well out of the medals and only finished ahead of the youngsters; that was it our Olympic games were over for another year.

But it was not just the Olympics we organised, I had refused to get involved in the school team, but I still needed that buzz of playing in organised football, it was ok having a kick about with your mates but I missed the thrill of competition.

This had got me thinking, we had our own estate Subbuteo League that we played in the summer months. Gary Lillyman had the best there was, it was fastened to a piece of hardboard and was as smooth as a baby's bottom.

I would hate playing in our house because the pitch would never stick to the carpet, this would also lead to you kneeling on a player and breaking him in half, on would come the trainer with his magic tube of glue and within no time he was back in action.

We played the games on our path and the biggest alarm clock in the world kept time, we had about eight kids in our league, Gary because it was his board had Sheffield Wednesday.

I cannot remember if anyone had the Blades, our Mark had Liverpool, while I liked the all-white strip of Leeds United; all the older lads had to flick their players but the young uns could drag their fingers now and again.

I would use a redundant school exercise book to work out the fixtures, you would each play seven games, we restricted this to two games each per day, and by the end of the week the league would be finished.

I don't think I ever topped the table but I enjoyed myself anyway, we would also visit Redgates the toy department store in town, they had the biggest Subbuteo collection in all the world, some sets had floodlights, and stands and spectators.

We would spend hours looking at the one they had on display, it was fantastic, how we would love that positioned on our block of houses, and we could still play when it went dark.

Those in charge of the store were not daft though, this section was in the basement, and unlike Woolworths on Waingate, you had three flights of stairs to negotiate if you ever felt like grabbing yourself Manchester United; I never pushed my luck in there, I could not afford to get caught again.

I got all the kids of the estate together and decided to form our own football teams, just like Subbuteo but this time instead of flicking little players, we would play the real thing.

I would organise one team which we called Newstead Park Avenue, Bryan Grayson would round up the kids on Newstead Way, Stephen Webster would take care of the Avenue and the Connealy brothers would make up the fourth, there was no age limit but you had to live on the estate to qualify.

We also operated along the lines of the sadistic school teacher and all the best players could not be all in the same team. What was the point of having a team that would win every game easily? It was to be seven a side and the games were all to be played on the school hockey pitch with its small goals. There would be two games every Sunday afternoon after we had all had our dinners.

Once the teams had been selected they all looked evenly balanced. We all met up to finalise the rules, and decided that the first games would take place in two weeks, we were also told that there was a stall in the Castle Market that sold very cheap football kits.

Terry and I went to check it out, there were piles and piles of shirts, socks and shorts of every colour imaginable. We reported back to the others and decreed that it was up to the individual player to finance his own kit.

Our team went for the green and black stripe, black shorts and green socks, the lads on the Way had blue shirts, white shorts and blue socks, the Connealy brothers had the all-white strip, and the Avenue boys had amber shirts, black shorts and black socks. How good did we look when we went up to the school fields on that very first Sunday? We were well ahead of our times, most of the games were evenly matched no one side took a thrashing, this was probably due to the fact the goals were small and the goalkeepers were good, we could not wait for the following Sunday to come along, kids started to go out of the house early doors just in case mum and dad wanted them to visit their close relatives.

At the end of the first round of games the team finishing bottom would be allowed to transfer a player from the team finishing top, this worked well because those selected and transferred just swapped kits.

We also didn't need the service of a referee, we policed our own games, we never allowed any tantrums like you have today, I also placed an advertisement in the Football Monthly magazine for friendly matches. I had loads of replies, but with the cost of travel out of the reach of our weekly budget, Crosspool was the furthest we could afford to travel.

We travelled and played on some school fields near to Manchester Road, and they returned the favour when they came over to play on Thornbridge School.

This would not happen today, unsupervised kids from the age of nine to thirteen taking themselves off to the other side of town just to enjoy a game of football.

Going back to Vic's planning department, they had provided us with a nice open space in the middle of the estate and placed no ball games signs, just in the right places to use as goal posts.

Back on the Rise, they had planted two trees so close together; they were also ideally placed for goal posts, much so that a plank of wood could be nailed temporally into position to create the acquired effect.

We would play this game called Wembley where you picked a team and once you had scored you were through to the next round, until it was whittled down to the last two, whoever got the last touch before it entered the goal would claim it.

Unfortunately this goal was right next to John Biggins's house, and if Dave Shirley let fly with one of his thunderbolts, it would have Mr Biggins running outside.

You see old Vic had once again failed to deliver and if the ball struck one of his manky grey tiles, they would break; the walls were that thin, the ball would remove anything that Mr Biggins had hanging on his wall.

Once he had come out that was the end of the game, we would move onto the garages that lined the road on Newstead Rise; the bottom and top ones we used as the goals, but they were made of metal and they would also make a racket when the ball hit them. This would have the old lady out and threatening to call the police if we didn't pack it in.

When it was freezing cold at night, old Vic had kindly left us a tap at the top of the garages and if you pressed down on it water would come flooding out, now we couldn't stand there all-night so we would place bricks on it to weight it down.

With a bit of luck the next morning we would have got our own personal skating rink. The ice could be an inch thick sometimes. The car owners were none too pleased. It was our very own toboggan run, we would have a great time until some mardy arse from the council would come and grit the road.

Sundays were great, all the kids would play on the estate or kick the ball about on the school fields, sometimes our games would be interrupted by that bastard on his motorbike, the dreaded Park Patrol whose job it was to terrorise the local kids who were doing no harm but play football or cricket on those school fields.

We used to run him ragged when he appeared, I don't think he ever caught anyone and our games would only be interrupted for a short while before he moved onto the next bunch of kids.

Another time that mum and dad were at Auntie Pat's we were again home alone, mind you the lads had been round all afternoon.

You see it was pissing it down outside and far too wet to play football outside, so with the quick arrangement of our furniture inside the Cronshaw stadium.

It was two a side football with a little plastic ball, our dining room chairs were placed one at each end of the room, while anything that looked like it may be breakable headed for the safe haven of the kitchen.

We knew we had a few hours to kill because they were never back before mid-evening;

well it was a right trek home after they had enjoyed a few sarnies and a sherry trifle.

I'll give old Vic Hallam his due; he made great big living rooms to enjoy kicking a ball around in, after we had rearranged all the furniture back into its rightful positions, the lads all went home.

We now settled down to enjoy a bit of the old Sunday evening light entertainment, we had been fed and watered and were enjoying the delights of the goggle box, when the bastard went off.

You see we had to deposit coins in the back of the damn thing to get it to work, now in the event of an emergency the neighbours would stump up the money if we were left in the dark.

So before going to see Mrs Batty we made sure all the lights were off and we were in complete darkness, I sent him across to beg for the money and in no time he had it in his grubby little hands.

Bingo, the lights were back on and we could see again, now we had the coins to bung in the television, result the box was again blaring out, we had only had it back on when this time the fucking lights did go out, we were plunged into darkness again, but this time we were not controlling the situation.

Again our kid was knocking on a neighbour's door, this time it was good old Shirley coming to the rescue; well we couldn't use Mrs Batty again.

In no time we had again restored the house to its former glory and just after nine mum and dad returned. I told mum straight away that the electricity had gone and we borrowed the money off Mrs Batty, she immediately sent us across with the money and all was well.

We thought it best not to tell her about the other money; she would probably get a little upset that we had been scrounging off the neighbours just to enjoy a bit of Morecambe and Wise.

We did get rumbled later on in the week when Shirley asked for her money back, and mums face was a little on the stern side when we returned from school.

She did shout a little bit, and with me being the oldest and wisest, I copped for the brunt of it, although that was lesson learned and we never pulled that stunt again.

The Final Countdown

When school broke up in July 1970, I knew that I had another cracking holiday lined up; you see Auntie Marjorie had moved to Morecambe years previous, and she offered our family free lodgings at her home.

She had a lad who was my age so I would be well catered for during our stay, Mark was now 10 years of age, and our David was just approaching his third birthday.

Mum decided that we needed a nice visit to the local barbers on Frecheville shops, and told us to take our David along with us; it was the time when the skinhead craze was all the rage.

So I decided to be a devil and settle for a moderate number two, it looked great so our Mark decided to follow suit, his lovely blonde locks were soon just a pile on the barber shop floor. Now what to do with this three year old whose wavy blonde hair made him look all girlish. I know long hair was the fashion back then and his looked great, but bugger it, in for a penny, in for a pound. Buzz went the clippers as they tore into his treasured locks, a couple of minutes later and they were joining his brothers' on the floor.

We looked the business as we munched on the sweets we'd bought with mum's change, we must have looked a picture has we walked through our estate, three little eggs in an egg cup, but one bigger than the other.

We walked down our path as Shirley next door was sweeping the path, the shock horror on her face as she shouted Marie come and look at your David, her face was a picture, what had we done to her little baby?

We had scalped him, she nearly burst into tears, I don't know what all the fuss was about, and it would have grown back next Whitsuntide when we would use him to fleece the neighbours.

Anyway the day had arrived and we trudged towards the bus stop, dad carrying that infamous white suitcase that had all the family clothes in. Once we got to Pond Street we waited patiently for the Morecambe bus.

While we were standing there, who should come waltzing down the platform but Granddad Sam. Mum's face was a picture because he and Marjorie had never got on while he was married to her sister Gertrude.

Sadly my Grandmother Gertrude had passed away earlier on in the year, another one of my guardian angels that had been taken too soon, I had not really got to know her like my other two angels, which was a crying shame really, but another good lady who had brought up her children in such trying times, and done a blinding job in the process.

What would she think when we turned up with Sam in tow, would she blame mum for bringing him after the death of her sister earlier on in the year? He must have thought it was time to see if her sister had mellowed towards him.

Well in about three hours we were about to find out as we all boarded the bus.

I don't really know what happened because as soon as we had landed I was off out with Trevor, he had two bikes that was quite handy and I helped him with his evening paper round.

He also had a canoe that we would carry to the artificial lake that appeared every time the tide went out, there was so much to do, what a place this was, and the next morning I helped him with his Sunday paper round.

But we made sure that our Mark didn't get his hands on them, well we didn't want Trevor getting the sack, Marjorie also enquired what had happened to our David's hair, had he been ill and lost it?

No she replied his brothers had him sheered just before we came away. Granddad Sam left on the Sunday and returned to Sheffield and everything was running smoothly until the Monday morning.

Marjorie's husband worked nights at the Post Office so she thought it best if we all go for a family stroll after breakfast. Off we all trotted except for our Mark who didn't want to go.

We had only gone a few hundred yards and Marjorie had forgotten her purse so dashed back to retrieve it. She returned minutes later dragging our Mark along, the little bugger had been going through her cupboards.

He said he was looking for a ball to play with but the adults were none too pleased with our kid, and although we enjoyed the rest of our stay in the seaside resort of Morecambe, our Mark put paid to any return visit for the foreseeable future.

It was also club trip time during the school holidays and this time thanks to Granddad Sam we had managed to get on another three outings, the first one we went on was the usual Pitsmoor Club trip, Dad was a lifetime member there and even though it was a drag to get over that side of the city, these trips were always enjoyable.

We also travelled on the yearly Sheffield Transport one; this was also a great day out where you would get a bag of goodies, a few shillings to spend and a fish tea before you returned home.

The best one though was the Manor Club seaside special; the coaches would line the length of City Road, we would get another little envelope that contained a few shillings, a nice drink of pop, fruit, bags of crisps and a sandwich. The destination was Cleethorpes with its mile upon mile of golden sands and deep blue sea.

I had our Mark in tow and we were kitted out in our lovely mustard jumpers again, we had enjoyed all that the east coast had to offer and we finished off the day with another fish dinner. We were playing football in that massive coach park again and the ball again went under one of the coaches.

We watched intently as this kid crawled under to retrieve the ball, when he reappeared you ought to have seen our faces, you are going to get murdered we told him.

It was his turn to get plastered with thick black grease, it must have come off the axle, and his best attire was ruined.

He also tried hopelessly to wash it off but it only made it worse; this time thankfully it was not me who was going to get it in the ear when the coaches disembarked in City Road.

August 1970 saw me heading in the direction of that place that got me my arsed tanned back in 1964, my mate from school Andy was a Unitedite and the Blades were playing Swindon Town.

I had money in my pocket so tagged along, I didn't fancy standing on the Shoreham Street end, so I made my way around to the Bramall Lane side of the ground, and coming towards me was my old mate Wesley.

He was wearing a white coat and carrying a tray, what you doing I enquired? His reply was that he sold refreshments from the tray and earn't himself a few bob.

He then proceeded to tell me that they were shorthanded and did I want a job? Andy wanted to watch the game so declined the invitation, but I was in like a shot. The old man who ran the show was not interested in any formalities, so I was advised to say that I was born in 1954 thus making myself nearly 16.

Soon I was kitted out and Wes was giving me a helping hand, I know we were not very good at maths in Junior School but he was well short of the mark with his calculations. I seemed to have one extra box of everything that was on my tray, it turned out that the first box was an added bonus. I followed Wes out onto the pitch side, he informed me that he never ventured into the mass of supporters because you'd get all your goodies lifted and stolen.

We worked like a dream team, back to back as we edged our way in front of the home fans, other kids would do the fetching and carrying to keep your tray well supplied.

I'd never seen as much money in my life, once the teams had taken to the field we made our way towards the away supporters, we would position ourselves on the cricket field so we could carry on serving the eager punters.

Once the half time interval was over, you had to report to the storeroom underneath the cricket pavilion. Kids were just lined up waiting to hand over their money, you also had to take into account your freebies and make sure that money was secreted in a nice little hiding place. Once you had paid in your takings he would give you your days wages.

I was now taking a keener interest in the home fixtures of Sheffield United, so once a fortnight I would be heading for the Lane, this also funded my trips to Hillsborough, and I was having the best of both worlds.

I had managed three home games and enjoyed Sheffield United funding my trips to Hillsborough, I was earning good money, but the best was yet to come with the visit of Sheffield Wednesday in October.

I had entered into my final year at school; I thought I would make their lives a misery this term.

I was getting ready into my battle fatigues, school trousers were on, and school socks were on, school shoes that were sponsored by Firth Browns were on and polished, my nice white shirt was tailored to perfection, and I really looked the business.

Now for the icing on this educational cake, I rummaged through my wardrobe, and pulled out three of Gertrude's finest, it was a struggle to choose but my dearly departed Grandmother had come up trumps with this canary yellow masterpiece.

I was now like a peacock as I strutted through this drab grey estate after feasting on a couple of Weetabix, I was ready to take on the world but in the meantime it was

Thornbridge School that was the enemy.

After the morning registration where I nearly blinded the teacher with the glow that was oozing from my chest, I made a beeline for the teacher who commented on my attire last term.

Give me a week and I'll have all the school wearing eye protectors, my mates were hysterical and loving every minute, we put our hearts and soul into the morning assembly, and it was fifteen minutes of pure joy.

I was dragged off to see the headmaster, they were none too pleased that I had opted for such an outlandish look, I was told to tone it down, I told them to get stuffed.

I had got to endure only eight more months in their company, so they had better get used to it, because it was the only clothes that I had suitable for my last throws of my educational life, so if they didn't mind I had a lesson to attend.

Gran had played a blinder, and this garment would be framed and sit proudly in my hall of fame, once my school days were over.

The powers that be came up with this great idea, lets introduce Social Studies into the curriculum. We were told to go out into the local community and see if we could offer a helping hand to our elderly who lived within walking distance to the school.

What great thinking, the teachers must have been laughing their bollocks off, yes let's get rid of the aptly named four set four, the ones who would be leaving come Easter 1971, let's throw them onto the educational scrapheap, they had not contributed anything in the previous academic year.

So in September 1970 we embraced this new lesson with great enthusiasm, the first task I entered into was making my very own map of the area; with just a notebook and pen and my trusty size nines, I marched up and down every road that was within, yes you have guessed it, walking distance of the school.

Then with the help of a giant piece of graph paper, I made myself my very own personal A to Z, I was very proud of what I had achieved, my masterpiece hung proudly on the classroom wall.

Our next project was to be our best yet, you see we called to the pensioners flats on Thornbridge Drive, and there lived an old lady called Mrs Henshaw.

She was great and we would sit chatting to her for ages, she lived alone and would always welcome our company every day after we had been left to our own devices.

One day while we were enjoying a nice cup of tea and a chat - the tea was great but she would always pass round these ginger nut biscuits, we were not being ungrateful but they were just not edible and it would take about a dozen flushes to send them deep down into the city's sewerage system.

Nigel came up with this great idea, lets decorate the old lady's living room, all those present which included myself, Bryan, Terry, Gary and Big John thought it was brilliant but would the school back our idea?

We thought this was another way we could all work together and get us ready to join the employment world in a few months' time.

Mr Mullen stumped up the cash to buy the necessary ingredients like paint, paste and wallpaper, while we all raided our family homes to bring the brushes and other tools of the trade.

In no time we had stripped her front room to the bare bones and the old lady had chosen the paper and colour scheme, Big John was left with the task of painting the ceiling, I don't think he needed any ladders; I bagged doing all the glossing, while Nigel, Bryan and Gary sorted out the wallpaper.

Mrs Henshaw manned the kettle to keep us topped up with tea, but I think she had taken hint with the biscuits because they were never forthcoming.

How proud were we when the job had been completed? It was probably the greatest thing I'd done in my life, Mr Mullen came down to view our handywork, and he also said that we had done a very good job.

We put him on the spot straight away when we suggested that we would like to complete the job by finishing the rest of the flat, which included the bedroom, kitchen and bathroom.

He said he would ask the powers that be if it could be funded, in the meantime I would like you all back in school.

Mr Mullen told us that before we left he was organising a school trip for us, and to fund this girls were busy baking cakes and buns, and selling them at break times.

But we were spending it on all the decorating products for the old lady, was this putting pressure on us to abandon our project so we could have a poxy day out?

What was the point in us attending school, we were doing more good in the community. I think some of the other kids were jealous that we had been able to swerve lessons and they were stuck in the boring classroom.

We did eventually get the go ahead to finish the job and the flat looked wonderful, only one thing was missing though the old lady didn't have a television.

In school the technically gifted pupils were working on this old black and white television, the science teacher could not believe that myself and Nigel were taking a keen interest in the restoration of this old dilapidated goggle box. Every spare minute we would sit intensely watching them tamper with it.

They were very good at what they did, because they soon had it, with the help of the good old science teacher, up and working. The picture wasn't too bad and the sound was great.

Boy did they slap each other on the back while leaving the science block, well done boys you have done a great job. When the coast was clear we gently passed the television through the now opened window where the rest of the gang had been waiting.

Off we shot over the back fields that ran onto Fox Lane; it weighed a bloody ton, it took an age to get it to Mrs Henshaws. Her face lit up like the Blackpool Illumination's when she saw it, we were also proud of what we had done.

I know it was technically stealing, but we had weighed up the options for the said television, one was spend the rest of your days in a grubby science classroom all alone after school had closed or spend it with a nice old lady in a warm newly decorated flat, and be lovingly polished once a week.

I know if I had been that bloody television, I'd have chosen flat number 3 on Thornbridge

Drive, wouldn't you?

We had laboured tirelessly over the past few months and all we had got to show for it was a few blisters and a head full of paint; someone who shall remain nameless managed to obtain a receipt book from the local do it yourself store though.

Sometimes the odd hooky receipt would find its way into the school office where it would be exchanged for the Queen's silver, then off the boys would shoot to town and play prize bingo on the gallery above the Pond Street Bus Station. If anything was forthcoming, Mrs Henshaw would buy the groceries off them.

Nigel and Richard also got cracking in the production of snow shovels, they would inform school that these were also our contribution to the care of the community, and were handed out free of charge, how gullible were they, our

motto was nothing in this life is free, and they had more willing customers once the snow started to fall.

Back on the football front Sheffield Wednesday had not played Sheffield United since January 1968, so the 3rd of October could not come quick enough; it was also going to be my best pay day of the season.

I was at the Lane bright and early, Wesley and I were in position long before the gates were open. We had again placed ourselves in our usual position and the money was flooding in, our helpers were working overtime bringing us more stock.

I must have sold more Wagon Wheels and cartons of pop in the past couple of hours than I'd done in all the previous home games, once the game started we eased off, I'd got pockets bulging with the Queens Silver, I had done ok!

But my football team were soon two goals down to our bitterest rivals, I was then nearly sending my tray skywards when we pulled it back to 2-2 before John Bloody Tudor hit the winner.

Never mind I consoled myself in the fact, that yours truly had fleeced them good and proper, and was onto a nice little earner.

At school things were ticking over, we had just enjoyed the Christmas and New Year break.

Once this was over, it was time to visit the careers advisor. She was a lovely lady who tried to steer me down the right road, and the school had already taken us on a visit to Brookhouse Colliery where we went underground, down we went inside the pit shaft before boarding a train to take us to the coal face. I hated every single minute of it, so a career down the mines was not for me.

Templeborough Rolling Mills had also been given the once over with all the noise and the dust it was nearly as bad as the bloody mine.

She asked me what I had done in school, what lessons I liked and had I made anything.

I told her about the house number plaque I had made in woodwork and the milk bottle holder I'd done in metalwork, I forgot to mention the horse racing game I'd lovingly created before Mr Russon had it cut up into little pieces.

We had managed a nice little cosy chat and she set me up with an interview at William Tyzacks at the bottom of the Moor.

The chap doing the interview was nice enough and seemed interested in my milk bottle rack seeing that this was an engineering company.

I liked this place until he took me onto the shop floor, again it was bloody noisy and dirty, and I was soon again losing interest in this profession and could not see myself stood at one of those machines day in, day out.

With my options limited I just did not know what I wanted to do, my mates seemed to have got all sorted out Bryan was heading for Brown Baileys, Nigel was going to be a mechanic with Ford's, Terry was also going to make a living in the motor trade.

I was adamant that the steelworks, mining or engineering was not for me, mum and dad were always on at me to get myself sorted because I would be leaving school in April 1971.

Mum had again put on the old weight and was pregnant again, another mouth was soon to be fed, but this time hopefully I would be helping to ease the burden on the family's finances.

Mum was probably hoping for a girl, with having four boys to look after which included my dad; her prayers were answered when on the 29th of March our Donna was born.

I now had a baby sister to add to my two brothers, mind you even before she was born, she had me scrapping. You see mum asked me to go to Mrs Smith who lived at the top of the Rise. She had sold my mum her old pram.

I was merrily pushing it home when two kids made disparaging remarks about my mum and dad being too old to be even contemplating having sex, never mind having a baby.

I just flew at them fists going like lightning speed, fucking hell they said calm down you bastard before someone gets hurt, don't you think you should retrieve your pram.

It was steadily making its way down the Rise, the chase was on once again but this time instead of it being that soppy poodle it was my mum's newly acquired pram, thankfully for me I got it back in one piece.

Granddad Sam had purchased the pram through a £3 loan to my Mum, unlike Gran he wanted paying back. During one family visit to his house he mentioned this in front of Auntie Pat and Uncle John while Uncle David and Auntie Carol were in attendance. He knew we were struggling financially but he had to have a dig.

Mum grabbed our Donna and left the house in tears, she walked all the way home and was still upset when she got back. Mum was a very proud woman and before the week was out that £3 had been returned in full, it must have stretched us to the limit but we survived.

It's a pity she didn't give me the shopping list so I could go out as the hunter gatherer, mind you knowing my luck I'd have only got caught.

Looking back it must have been bloody hard trying to cope and maintain the household on a shoestring budget; I would help with the weekly shop accompanied by my Mum of course and love it on the return when the biscuit barrel was full to bursting.

Don't forget they have got to last until next Friday and once they have gone that's it.

Times were hard but we were loved and Mum always had a cooked meal waiting for us every teatime; one Sunday when she was heavily pregnant with our Donna, she'd busied herself early morning with the traditional cooked English breakfast, after we'd all been fed and watered we vacated her domain the kitchen and made ourselves comfortable in the living room.

Dad had his head in the Sunday paper and was oblivious to all the commotion coming from behind the kitchen door, then one really flustered lady appeared in the doorway.

Jim can I have an hand in the kitchen, was it too much to ask, I've cooked a lovely breakfast and managed to wash all the pots singlehandedly and now I'm well on the way into preparing the Sunday dinner.

Dad then made the mistake of his life, in a minute he responded and a pan of finally nurtured Brussels sprouts were heading in his direction.

Boy was that funny, he jumped up in a threatening manner but it was all bravado, he stood no chance against this Manor lass, I mean she stood up to Grandma Flo so Dad was cannon fodder.

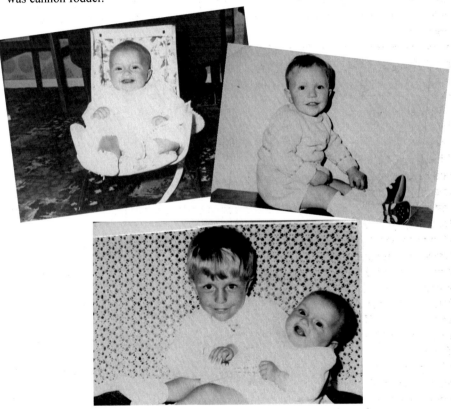

Now we had another mouth to feed, I was leaving school in about a week's time, yet I had not fixed myself up with a job. The rest of the lads were enjoying the Easter break knowing full well that on the 19th of April 1971 they would be heading not back to school but clocking on at their respective jobs.

I'd got nine days to sort myself out; I had even been shown the door from Bramall Lane because some policeman had felt my collar for working under age, it was the home game with Bolton Wanderers that they were doing checks and I was only about two weeks away from my fifteenth birthday and I'd been rumbled.

They took my tray and white coat off me and booted me out of the ground; the miserable bastard did not even let me watch the match.

On Easter Monday I went to Hillsborough to witness the Owls and Blades fight out a 0-0 draw, fighting at football was now common place but as of now I was not involved.

After the Easter festivities had ended I made my way into town and wandered into the fish market. I was looking if there were any jobs to be had. I knew one or two lads at school had Saturday jobs helping out for a few quid but would this place be ripe for full time employment?

After an eventful but non productive day I called time on my job hunt, I needed to get my finger out and find something. At this moment in time I was thinking why had I not taken Mr Tyzacks up on his offer of an apprenticeship?

I was really down in the dumps and knew that mum would be on my case and rightly so, I could have had a job lined up but it was just not for me.

Schools out for Ever

I walked down Dixon Lane and I noticed a sign in the window of W J Kings, it read Bacon Assistant wanted. I walked in off the street and asked to speak to the manager. He was located up a flight of stairs, he was enjoying a break and asked if I fancied a cup of tea. We sat chatting over a brew. I must have impressed him because he offered me the job there and then.

I would start first thing Monday morning and my wage would be a whopping £9 a week. I rushed home to tell the family I had got myself a job, mum was pleased for me, so much so that she would let me keep my first week's wage before I started paying board. I was also on nearly double what those who had taken up an apprenticeship were on.

Even though work was only days away we were still doing what we had been doing during our schooldays.

Playing football and just hanging around on the streets, we were the original inbetweeners, too old to be doing stuff that kids did, but not yet old enough to enjoy the pubs or the X-rated cinema.

I was fifteen, still really a kid. Even though I hated the final years of my schooling I loved my schoolmates, we had fought the system and took them to the cleaners. They treated us as second or even third class citizens, what were they thinking of when they scrapped our two tier education system?

The final weekend of my freedom was spent on the Sunday lazing on the school fields enjoying the top forty after playing football for the past few hours; this was rudely interrupted by the motorbike riding Park Patrol.

We scattered in all directions; this was the last thing I needed getting my collar felt by the crazy bike rider, who was backed up by a couple of patrol cars. Had the bastards not got anything better to do on this lazy Sunday afternoon?

We leapt the fence and headed for the fields that led to Birley Woods. Terry had raced back to retrieve the tranny radio, relaxing in the relative safety of the woods we just carried on chilling out, the morning would see us all going our separate ways, no more would we sit in class or sing hymns at the school assembly.

Well the day had come. I left the house at 8am to catch the bus into town. I know I was going to work but I still paid the child fare, on my arrival I was met by the shop manager and two lads that were a lot older than me.

I was wearing a nice shirt but no tie, a nice pair of black trousers and new shoes. I could see them sniggering, I know I was the new kid but their reception was a bit frosty, just like that bloody fridge.

A big lorry then pulled up outside the shop, it was our weekly meat supply and they told me to get outside.

About five minutes later they joined me, they were dressed up like American footballers, side after side of bacon was handed down by the lorry driver and they were piss wet through.

There was a knack to carrying these and I was having a torrid time, once inside the fridge you had to reach up and place the hook onto the rail, they made it look so easy.

I was doing ok but they could see by now I was struggling, then disaster; I missed my footing and finished up in a heap in the fridge with the side of bacon wrapped around my neck.

They were laughing their bollocks off at my expense, the bloody bacon was covered in sawdust and I was soaked from head to foot in bacon fat.

Welcome to the world of bacon produce, they finished off unloading the van while I tried to dry myself the best I could. You see they had removed their shirts and were wearing about five white coats.

We sat together upstairs and they'd even made me a nice warming cup of tea, it was a kind of initiation ceremony that bestowed every newcomer. Give me a break boys, I was only 15 and weighed in at about nine stones.

W J Kings was a well-established Sheffield company and had quite a few shops in the area, apart from ours there was another one further down Dixon Lane, Pinstone Street and at the bottom of the Moor.

Now they set about the task of teaching me how to bone bacon and cut cheese. Because I was the new lad I got to get all the ribs out of the sides of bacon, this was done by snicking round the top of the rib with a very sharp knife, then placing a loop of string around it before pulling on it. Once you got the knack they came out easy, it did take the skin off your hands though by the time you had finished the last one.

This was the worst job and it was mine all mine. After every side was bone free you had to replace it on the rail in the fridge before moving onto the next, I was bloody knackered as we shut up the shop at 5.30pm.

I think once I got home I had my tea and went straight to bed. The following day it was a lesson in cutting all the cooked meats, corned beef, boiled ham, veal, stuffed pork and tongue.

This I mastered in no time and I made sure that I kept my fingers well away from the circling blade; after this was done I was shown how to clean the machinery without removing my fingers.

You never seemed to have a free minute to yourself; there was always something that needed doing, one time the lads told me to put on this white coat over my other one, I was expecting another bacon delivery but once it was fastened they grabbed me and proceeded to hang me by a couple of hooks on the bacon rail, not only was I up in mid-air the bastards had locked me in the fridge.

I was in there for ages and non-too pleased when the bullying bastards let me out, I took this banter for what seemed like an age until one of the twats took it a step too far - they had filled my brand new shoes with bacon fat.

I never had much as a kid, and looked after my possessions. I flew downstairs and started swinging at the ginger ugly bastard. He was bigger, stronger and older than me but who cared.

I was having him, the other lad pulled him off me and he was still giving it large, I thought for a minute of picking up a knife and slicing him but that would have made me the coward.

From that day the bullying stopped; the banter and the practical jokes continued but nothing malicious or threatening.

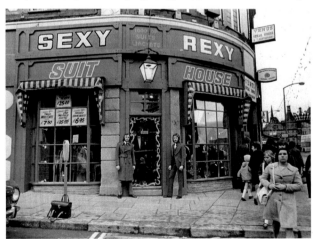

Mum was true to her word and my first weeks wage of £9 was mine all mine, the first thing I purchased was a nice pair of Levi jeans and a Brutus shirt with buttoned down collars; the irresistible Ben Sherman would have to wait. A nice pair of Brogues finished off my wages and meagre savings.

I purchased my clothes from Sexy Rexy, no Barney Goodmans for this follower of fashion, it was like an Aladdin's cave inside, and I would spend most of my dinner time just browsing the latest fashion that was hitting the High Street.

I worked from Monday to Saturday and had half a day off on a Thursday, so Sunday was the only full day I had all to myself. I was still knocking about with my school friends Bryan Grayson, Terry Loukes, John Ashforth, Stephen Webster and Gary Drury. Mr Fiddler was right though, he told us before we were leaving that contact with our former classmates would be minimal. We told him he was talking nonsense, we had been friends for the past three years and some of the lads had known one another since they were five years old.

How could we break our ties as easy as that?

There were nearly eighty lads in our year, out of them we had a good twenty five that would play and congregate on our estate in one form or another and now within a couple of months of leaving school, we had dwindled to a mere six.

We met on the estate and our dress was very smart and our hair was neat and tidy, the skinhead dress code had moved on we were more of the suede head variety; mind you none of us had ever really adopted the look of the skinhead, and the animosity it attracted.

I'd seen these lads at the football and hanging around the bus station in Pond Street, they look really menacing. Nigel and Gary would tell of them causing trouble at the Top Rank on a Tuesday night, the security that policed the place would not allow them to enter the building but they would wait outside and give grief to anyone who crossed their path.

Times were a changing for me and I now had money in my pocket.

It was also coming in on a weekly basis and no one could take it away from me, no teacher, no newsagent, and no policeman like it had happened in the past.

The only person who could fuck it up was me and I was not going to do that.

The summer of 1971 and we were off to Cleethorpes. As we boarded the train at the Midland Station we managed to get a carriage all to ourselves, we had pulled the top of the window apart to let in some fresh air, the weather was gorgeous.

Big John was outside in the corridor, he liked to put his massive frame through the open door window. We had been told as kids to never do this because a passing train would have our heads off.

But now we had no parents in attendance to tell us what to do we were in complete control; again no one in authority had a control over us, as long as we were on our best behaviour.

Anyway the time flew by and we were soon moving through the outskirts of Grimsby as the train neared our destination, and boy did these 15 year-old something's look smart.

We were in jovial mood as the train came to a sudden stop, off we shot and as I glanced around I noticed that none of us were minus our heads; the scare tactics that we had encountered all these years were just a fallacy.

We moved through the ticket barrier and had our tickets clipped, must remember to put them safe for the return journey.

On leaving the station it was wall to wall with big looking and menacing bikers, there were bikes everywhere.

They were laughing their bollocks of at us, I was wishing my hair was down to my knees and I had got a nice leather jacket on.

We jumped down the remaining few steps and headed for the amusements, everywhere we turned it was full of bikers, the only place we could not see a bike and leather jacket was the beach.

It was suggested that we made for the safe haven of the sands, we were now in a bike free zone and John immediately pulled out a knife.

I thought what is he doing carrying that, was he looking for trouble? Was he carrying on this skinhead tradition of seeking confrontation with the rockers or bikers? No the big daft lump just wanted a game of stretch.

This was a game where you made your opponent stretch his legs to bursting point but the knife must land upright and secure in the ground; the only way to stop this from happening was to land the knife between your opponent's legs.

Trouble was though the sand was that soft the knife stuck in every time, we soon got bored.

John was told to put his knife away and keep it hidden for the remainder of the day.

Cleethorpes must be the only seaside resort that you nearly had to walk home to locate the sea; it was miles out before we even got the whiff of the salt water.

We did manage to paddle our feet in the sea before we became bored yet again. It was a long walk back to civilisation, and the roar of the motor bikes were getting louder by the minute.

I had had enough, I needed to enjoy the amusements before I caught the train home. We headed for the big arcadia with its dodgems and waltzer. I was determined to enjoy the final couple of hours doing what I wanted to do.

I was oblivious to those big hairy bikers; I was ramming all-comers on the dodgems, while over on the waltzer I was making sure my loose change didn't fly out of my pocket, this I knew to do from experience.

You see every year a fair would visit Sheffield 12, and position itself at the bottom of Fox Lane. I was on the waltzer one night and enjoyed about three minutes of being thrown about and spun a thousand times.

It was great, the trouble being that when I got off, I was penniless; I knew that the money had fallen out of my pockets and must have gone down the back of the seats.

I asked this kid operating the ride if I could retrieve my money, is answer was short and brutal.

No you can't so fuck off.

I did not like his attitude so borrowed the price of a ride off Bryan, I bided my time and waited my chance, and the gobby bastard had been replaced by another lad, so I went for it.

I got into the carriage and lifted the seat, fucking hell it was like a goldmine, no wonder he told me to fuck off, the seat was minted.

I grabbed and grabbed, then grabbed some more, I was stuffing coin after coin into my trouser pocket, Bryan said that the kid was getting ever closer collecting the money but it was too late we were off, we had vacated the carriage and were off.

We even left the seat up to show they had been rumbled, the bastards were none too pleased and I really flaunted it, my pockets were bulging, and I stood there shaking them, and they couldn't do a thing about it.

The place was rammed with people and the local bus stop was just across the road, the lads thought I was pushing my luck, because the fairground kids had a right reputation for handing out a few slaps.

I had made a right killing and was very pleased with myself, I never returned to the fair that year; I had made my point, and lived to tell the tale.

I had now been employed for six months, the bullying and trick playing had stopped, I would now help out on the serving department, the decimal system made this easy, even though I hated maths at school this was enjoyable.

With Christmas just around the corner I visited Suggs and laid away the greatest present, not for me but for our Mark, it was a Subbuteo set. We had never had one as kids so now was the perfect opportunity.

A bit of an arterial motive, well he did need someone to play with.

I had another new workmate, the bully had left and this lad from Frecheville called John joined us. He had dyed hair, a kind of reddish colour, he was a right music fanatic and would tell of all the concerts he had been too.

John was great to work with and going to the job every morning now became enjoyable, I would go with him in our dinner hour, around the market and we would look through all the second hand records.

He also dressed the part in his platform shoes and even got me to purchase a pair of bib and brace trousers that I wore with my very own platforms at the Gary Glitter concert at the City Hall.

He was more into David Bowie and Roxy Music, but at present it was Glitter, Sweet and Slade that I was into.

At work I had moved on now from being just the old bacon lad and would serve the customers when we were busy. I loved the responsibility of being left to mind the shop when the manager was out, I had been placed in trust and at no time did it enter my head to help myself to anything that was not mine, I was growing up, and acting as such.

We were soon joined by another member of staff called Ray; he was the one who introduced me to the horses, I know I'd watched my dad gamble away every Saturday; he was the inspiration behind my lucrative gambling game.

On a Saturday I would study the form from the morning paper and have my 22p at the ready, I would stake this in a 6-4-1 or Yankee as it was called, 6 doubles, 4 trebles and an accumulator.

I would write it out on my betting slip and Ray would take all the bets, I would always pay my tax on it which I think was around 3p. Ray loved his gambling and even set up this pontoon on the football when you got a team and it was the first to score 11 goals, the money in that jar would increase weekly, everybody in the shop had a go, even some of the regular customers.

We would mark the chart in the room upstairs and if you scored more than 11 you would go back to 7, until the money was finally won. We were now in the age of the decimal coins; it was now 100 pennies to the pound.

It made life easier for us but for the old folk visiting the shop it was a nightmare. It had been brought in on the 15th of February 1971, at school they had given us plastic coins to practice using them. The banks of this country had closed their doors on the previous 10th at 3.30pm and had not re-opened until 10am on the 15th.

This allowed them time to stock up on the new money; the five new pence and the ten had been introduced in April 1968 because they were the same size and weight as the shilling and two shilling respectively.

A year later in October 1969 the fifty new pence was introduced while in November 1970 the old ten bob note vanished forever.

It was now the summer of 1971 and the old folks of this city had a purse and pocket full of these new coins; the new half penny, the one and two pence, the five and ten, plus finally the fifty. I'm sure they thought we were short changing them every time they entered the shop.

I was enjoying work and my home life was good; mum was kept busy with the new baby and our David was just about ready to start his schooling, while Mark was eleven and embarking on his final year in junior school before moving up to that horrible Thornbridge Comprehensive.

It was now his turn to get the family into the spotlight, we had decided that the regular Sunday trip over to Brinsworth was not our cup of tea for this soon to be sixteen year old and the younger sibling at eleven.

It was a right pain in the arse though, three bloody bus journeys just to get there and enjoy a few spam sandwiches a couple of cakes and a bowl of trifle.

Me and our Mark were now getting older and started to swerve the traditional Sunday expedition and we were left to fend for ourselves.

Mum realised just like she had when she swerved the Garnhams on the Parson Cross that we were growing out of going.

One time I was busy cutting up the potatoes to have some lovely rustic chip sandwiches for tea when young Batty came running in the house, your Mark has gone and fell out of the trees on Birley Lane. Well I replied tell him to be careful then, no he has fell out onto the bonnet of a car.

He had gone and fallen onto the bonnet of a car that was travelling up the lane and thankfully the driver was not speeding, our kid got a head injury because the startled driver slammed on the brakes and he fell off the bonnet.

Somebody had called for an ambulance and whisked our Mark off to the hospital; I now needed to firstly check if I had turned the chip pan off before going in the search of mum and dad.

Mr Batty took me in his car to locate mum and dad and trust me to go to the wrong grandparent first when I went all the way to the bloody Kelvin flats, poor old Florence Emily had seen her lovely house on Hoyland Road erased to the ground. The bloody council had placed her in the so called streets in the sky.

I was now heading back to the Manor before discovering that they were at neither of these places but down at Auntie Pat's at Brinsworth.

When I had finally tracked them down we all shot off to the Children's Hospital to find out what had happened to that trainee stunt man brother of mine.

Our kid you see was only 11 and I was fifteen but this bitch who they had alerted from the social services was giving mum the bloody third degree and slamming her for leaving us home alone, she told mum that if this happened again she would be reporting her to the powers that be.

Mum had to bite her lip and contain herself from giving it her back, yes we were really neglected, and scratching around in bins because we were so undernourished, how thick must she had been, or was she one of those kids who loved the Sunday visit to the relatives, and then spend the next five hours bored to tears while you could be playing with your mates.

Bet she had got no friends the stuck up cow I thought.

Nobody got the blame for letting our Mark climb the bloody tree, he was eleven and it's what kids of his age did, nothing came of it and a few weeks later they were back up those bloody trees.

I was earning good money, nearly double what the lads were earning, so I put it to good use, I would browse my mum's club book and knew that whatever I wanted I could have.

I just had to divide the total cost by twenty, also one of the ladies at work also ran one, so if ever mum put a limit onto what I was spending I could always swerve her and purchase from the good lady at work.

My very first purchase was for a full set of fishing tackle; I wasn't mad on the sport but knew that the nearby pond at Frecheville could be visited when the weather was nice.

I think I had only used it twice during my first five weeks of payment but as I had said earlier, I wasn't a fanatic when it came to the fishing.

Mark told of a forthcoming trip to the ponds at Clowne and all his mates were going.

He was the only one without any tackle so could he borrow mine? I didn't object, what harm could it do; even though he had previously got me the sack from my paper round I bore no grudges.

I put the tackle out for him as I went to work that Saturday morning, the rod, the basket and all the accessories were neatly stacked by the front door. Just after nine o'clock, his mates from the estate came calling, mum had packed him up some sandwiches and a drink, they ventured down to the Four Lane Ends to catch the green bus that headed for the ponds.

They must have had a right old day with the fishing because he had not returned home when I got in from work, nor had he arrived before I went out with the lads to the local Rex cinema.

When I returned home from the pictures he was fast asleep, he looked completely knackered but so was I.

When I awoke the next morning he had already gone out to play, I went down stairs and mum was preparing one of her special cooked English breakfasts.

I noticed though that there was no sign of my fishing tackle, bloody hell he must be keen if he's gone fishing again as I sat down to enjoy my bacon and eggs. Mum eventually broke the bad news.

That brother of mine had enjoyed the fishing that much it must have affected his brain. You see sitting on your arse all day, trying to catch Moby Dick, must play havoc with your memory.

He managed to collect all the gear off the bankside and put it away neat and tidily, he also managed to cart it all to the bus stop. That is when his problem set it in you see. When the bus eventually arrived he was in such a hurry to get on board that the sod forgot to grab the fishing tackle.

Once he had remembered, himself and one of his mates jumped off the bus, while the rest of them carried on their journey home. The two little buggers ran all the way back to the bus stop outside the pond but the fishing stuff had vanished.

They had to wait ages for another bus and that's why he was not back when I got home from work.

I had only made a quarter of those weekly payments and only used it twice and now it was gone, that really put an end to my days on the high seas, I don't think I ever went fishing again.

The catalogue or club book was great though, it enabled Mum and Dad to purchase an array of items that could be paid back on the weekly.

A new washing machine and gramophone cabinet were one of their early purchases, mum had now got a part time job, and if dad was at work at the same time, I would look after the kids while Shirley kept an eye on our Donna.

Shirley had three kids of her own, Dougie who attended Firth Park, that also was once a grammar school, Mark was about the same age as our David and Gillian,

I opened my very first savings account at the post office on the Frecheville shops, I had deposited a princely sum of two pounds and I banked on being able to save a pound a week.

I wasn't really into the pubs just yet, mind you we probably would not get served, after finishing work we would still play football on the estate. Everyone would talk about their day at their respective jobs, and we would just laze about in the evening summer sunshine.

A couple of the boys had carried on their dirty habit of smoking that they had started in school, but this was not for me, I'd tried it once behind the sheds at school but hated it. It was just a waste of money.

Sunday was great for me. I didn't have to go to work, my mates only worked from Monday to Friday, and we would meet up and play football while the older lads would be heading for the pub which opened their doors at twelve o'clock.

While they were guzzling the beer in the two hours that it was open, we had headed for our old school fields to kick that ball about; it seemed that we were stuck in a time warp.

Mum would still cook that traditional Sunday roast, and that was soon disappearing off my plate.

I would chill for the remainder of the day before carrying on that great tradition of having a nice soak in the bath while listening to the top forty.

The music that introduced the Alan Freeman pick of the pops show, it would start at four o'clock and last for three hours before they announced the number one just before seven. If I was not in the bath, I would be on the school field with the old transistor blasted out the latest offerings that the good people of this country would be buying. One such record that made me chuckle was Chirpy Chirpy Cheep Cheep by Middle of the Road, this made number one in July 1971. One line in the record asks where your mamma gone, little baby son; were they singing about our Mark back a decade, when his mamma had done a disappearing act and moved on.

It was around this time that the Newstead and Weaklands Tenants Association was founded, the rumour had it that they were planning to set up a football team to play Saturdays.

But they needed funding, the committee decreed that if we helped out with the fund raising they would sanction the team, they decided to run a tote draw once a week.

We were set the task of knocking on every door in the neighbourhood to get people to part with their cash.

It was soul destroying at first because no one seemed interested in having a go. Door after door was slammed into our faces. We went to every single house on the estate and the lads from over the road on the Weaklands had done the same.

The winning prize was more than most people earned in a week, it snowballed from that first draw and now everyone wanted a piece of the action. All those involved had a list of customers and you had to have the money in by the draw which was held every Thursday at 7.30pm.

If you knocked on the door and got no answer that was tough, they would miss out. The cash was rolling in and a football kit was purchased and the Newlands Football Club was founded. The colours were yellow and blue, the association also had premises behind the shops on the Birley, we helped decorate and paint it, and in return it became our little meeting house.

It was where we could partake in the odd tin of beer, it was like our very own youth club. But after all our hard work raising funds for the football team, we were kind of pushed to one side because the older lads from both estates made up the bulk of the players, we never got a look in, so it was decided to form another team for the younger lads.

And we had managed to get into the under 18 league that the Sheffield and Hallamshire had just started, this also created a problem because our oldest players were just turned 16 and the youngest were 14, we roped Mr Biggins in to be our manager.

Well we did promise to stop playing outside his house if he took up the challenge; we played on the field adjacent to Westfield School and would either change on the school premises or in the Queens public house.

This was great because the landlord would sometimes serve us the odd pint if we were good. If we were good we were terrible, I don't think we ever won a game all season and finished up pointless at the end of it all.

Mind you we had enjoyed ourselves along the way.

There was also another team on the estate that was run by David Shirley's dad, they were called Birley Boys but none of us were good enough to get into that team. They were self-funded and this upset Mr Shirley that his lads never got any help from the tenants association.

I had just celebrated my 16th birthday, it was November 1971, it was now the opportunity to try pastures new on the public house front, we had managed the odd summer pint in and around the village of Ridgeway; the Queens, White Swan and further down the valley the Bridge at Ford would wet our whistle.

Big John would do the honours and he would reappear with four or five pints of lager and lime; I hated the taste of bitter, that must be back from the days of sitting outside the Five Arches waiting for closing time so I could walk home with Grandma and Granddad, if anyone had left any dregs in the bottom of the glass, we would have a taste.

It was horrible, how could they sit in these places?

Sometimes there would be more smoke coming out of them than our den on the Shirecliffe tip; we would sometimes open the lounge door to gaze into this adult world, every chair would have an occupant and the noise would be deafening as all those seated would natter away like there was no tomorrow.

Gran would be sat at the very same table, week in week out; I would try in vain to attract her attention in the hope that a few pence would be coming my way and I could visit the off sales for a nice little box of chocolate peanuts or raisins.

The best we got was when it was closing time and she treated me to a nice bag of piping hot chips with scraps on, lashings of salt and vinegar. I would drown the bastards in the tangy dark liquid, you had to blow and blow on every single one, they were that hot, rustic brown in colour just like Gran's toast.

I would think back about those days as I sipped on my lager in the summer sunshine.

Terry told of the Centre Spot on the Basegreen estate; it was running topless go-go dancers every Sunday night, and he thought we should try our luck.

It was not like a mental Saturday night in the area where all the nutters from the area would descend on the local pubs that had discos on, the worst place for trouble was the Birley Hotel.

That had a reputation second to none. It would have bands on or a disco every Saturday night and you avoided this place at all costs; gangs of men would travel from all the neighbouring estates, Hackenthorpe, Woodthorpe, Basegreen and the Manor, plus you would get all the locals from Birley and Frecheville.

It was a recipe for violence, they were all after the same thing, alcohol, a good time and the ladies, you mix all this together and it is bound to lead to trouble. All these rival factions would be banded together in the very large concert room and one wrong push or spilt drink could lead to something that resembled a good old fashioned bust up that you would see in any old saloon in the old wild west.

It was not only this public house that was on our places to avoid list, there was the Elm Tree at the Manor Top, the Woodthorpe a little bit further down Mansfield Road and last but not least was the Old Harrow at Gleadless; this pub too attracted its fair share of trouble, they too had bands and the disco on, it also attracted the same explosive clientele so for the time being we preferred the more tranquil surroundings of the village of Ridgeway.

So it was settled then, we would grace the Spot this Sunday, we knew that the pub would not open its doors until 7pm, and we didn't want to be first through the doors, so it was decided we would meet at 8pm and make the short journey over Birley Lane to the Basegreen estate, this was the first ever time we had tried anything like this.

Would we pass for eighteen, would we get served, or would we get our heads kicked in as we got to the bottom of the lane; a steady stream of people were heading for the nearby Old Harrow.

But as for now that was out of our league, we got closer and closer and could hear the faint noise of the disco blaring out. Now the place was upon us, we entered the concert room door and result, the lights were off; it was only the beams of the disco lights that were illuminating the place.

Terry got sat at this table at the rear of the room while Bryan and Big John went to the bar, I joined Gary and Terry and it was so far so good.

The place was quite busy but not heaving like the Harrow or the Birley which was good on our part because this landlord was trying something new and it needed paying for.

So our money was as welcome as anyones, we now felt like adults enjoying the adult world, and why shouldn't we? All of us were working, all of us could now legally smoke and get married but we couldn't have a beer.

I think this was also the first time we bought rounds of drinks, mind you Bryan and John had the honours of buying them.

The atmosphere was jovial, I think the flowing of the old amber nectar with the dash of lime was doing the trick, the company was great, the place was great, and not one hint of any trouble.

The star of the show came on late into the evening, she was gorgeous, and my oh my, could she dance, unfortunately for the good lady it was not her dancing that interested us, it was her massive tits.

She was only yards away from us, she had moved off of the stage and was circling the audience, and they were much appreciative, the ladies in the audience were none too pleased, as their husbands and boyfriends latched their eyes on that rounded pair of breasts.

What a night we had encountered, what was all the fear about? We did though leave before the end, before the lights came on; we wanted to return so no point in pushing our luck. We were really on a high as we walked home, I think the five, yes five, pints were starting to have the desired effect, I had never drunken as much in my whole life and as I finally said farewell to my mates, the best in the world I shouted, I made for our door.

I think the key was not working, it took me ages to open the damn thing, once inside I made the fateful decision to say goodnight to mum and dad. My dad's face was a picture, he knew I was drunk, and probably knew also that I would not get my usual good night's sleep.

I was soon upstairs and into bed, I lay on my back and stared at the ceiling, the covers weighed a ton, I needed to remove them, they were choking me, next minute the light was spinning around like it was on the fairground waltzer, what was happening, only two hours previous I was having the time of my life, now I was gasping for air.

I needed the toilet, my head was deep inside the bowl, probably just as deep as Christopher's was back in junior school, but unlike him, I wanted mine in there, I was being violently ill, I was throwing up for England.

I was now starting to feel sorry for myself, were all the beer guzzling teenagers around the country doing this after they had enjoyed their night out? I must have visited that toilet about a dozen times during the night.

I felt shocking when I awoke in the morning, I must have cleaned my teeth an umpteen times, but could I not rid myself of that horrid taste in my mouth.

I swerved any form of breakfast, all the kids were up and it was like feeding time at the zoo, not even the offer of a special brew of mum's favourite tea could bring me around. Off out of the door I went, it was pissing it down. I was feeling as bad as the weather. All the way along Newstead Road I trudged, passing Terry's house, and I wonder what the rest of them were feeling like.

I queued with the rest of the passengers at the bus stop on the top of Occupation Lane and waited for the number 41, the Hackenthorpe flyer to transport me to work. I paid my junior fare of 2p, thus saving myself 8p on the adult fare.

I didn't fancy standing up so ventured upstairs into the smoke filled atmosphere of the top deck, if I was not feeling bad enough, I had to breathe in the fumes of the Park Drive brigade.

Then to bring the curtain down on the most dismal day in my entire life I heard those immortal words of tickets please, fucking hell I'd only paid a two, I fumbled into my pocket and pulled out a solitary 10p piece, that's all I had on me.

The inspector inched his way down the bus, looking at every single ticket. I glanced down at my attire, I had been in such a rush I was not wearing my schoolboy look, no black blazer, no white shirt and tie, I was fucked.

That uniform look had saved me a fortune over the past six months, fucking Blakey, had sussed me out, and demanded I paid the adult fare, the bastard took my last solitary 10p piece, I was potless as I alighted in Pond Street.

How was I going to get home? That would have to wait because when I turned the corner into Dixon Lane I was met with the sight of our bacon delivery, that's all I needed, those bastard pigs drooling all over me in the state I was feeling.

I walked in through the door and climbed the stairs. Arthur the shop manager, John and Ray were having a cuppa, the three of them in unison said that I didn't look well, and what was the matter.

I probably could have blagged it and been sent home but I knew I would get it in the neck from mum if I did, I was honest with them from the off, it was self-inflicted I commented. I had got drunk for the first time in my entire life and was not feeling 100%.

John and Ray were diamonds; they covered for me all day, unloaded the bacon, boned most of it, and did most of the spring clean we did every Monday, what a contrast these two were from the other two bullying bastards who had gone to pastures new.

I missed out on my dinner, I told them I was not hungry, I was fucking starving but I was skint, I hated borrowing anything.

At the end of the day when we finally closed the shop I made my excuse to John that I was not going home just yet I had something to do, you see we usually caught the same bus home and I had no bus fare.

As he went to catch the bus I headed for Duke Street to make that steady climb to the Manor Top, what an end to a shocking day.

This time yesterday I was having a nice soak in the bath, listening to the latest charts, and that priceless introductory music from Alan Freeman's pick of the pops, now I was wet again but this time I had my clothes on.

It took me ages to reach the summit, only Mansfield and Birley Moor Roads to go and I was nearly home. It was well turned seven o'clock when I got home and I was drenched.

To bring this very sad day to a conclusion, my tea was frazzled in the oven; I must have been in bed for eight.

I was a new man when I awoke Tuesday morning and could not wait to visit the Spot again this forthcoming Sunday and have my fill of ale and breasts.

We were now spending more time in the pubs at the weekend; it was mainly Sunday with me because I never got home from work on a Saturday night until after 7pm.

I even missed out if the lads tried to get into the Rex to see a mucky film, that usually included the delightful Ingrid Pitt, getting the blood sucked out of her while flashing them lovely tits, all the rage during this period was the horror/sex movie which also included Vincent Price and Peter Cushing, they were the guvnors when it came to the old fright night.

Christmas was now upon us, it was to be my first ever as a working adult. I had been paying weekly at Suggs for my present for our Mark. Why I was buying him anything was beyond me, he had lost all my fishing tackle the previous summer, but I had forgiven him.

I hated fishing anyway, it was a Subbuteo that I was getting him. Well we never had one as kids so I was getting him something that we could all involve ourselves in, I cannot really remember what I bought for the rest of the family.

In the run up to the festive period I was working nonstop, we were really busy at work, while all my mates had been given two weeks off because they worked in the steel industry; I had to work until half past five on Christmas Eve.

I enjoyed Christmas Day and Boxing Day off before returning to work the following day, this was to be repeated the following week when I had to work until tea time on New Year's Eve.

1972 and I was spending more time at home than going out, you see my wages just did not stretch to living the high life, one trip to the pictures, one mid-week football match and the pub on a Sunday evening had me penniless.

While those who had chosen the steel industry course like Bryan were now enjoying good money, their work was dirty and tough, and they were rewarded greatly for it. He also had suffered an initiation ceremony when he was finally attached to a department, the older blokes stripped him of all his clothes, set the hosepipe on him and then rolled him into the sand, the sand was so rough it nearly took all his skin off, and he was itching like mad, they removed most of the sand by turning the hosepipe back on him, after enduring this he was welcomed into the team and became a valuable member.

By February the country was grinding to a halt, the miners were on strike and well over a million workers had either been laid off or were on a three day week.

Those who opted for the steel and engineering industries were feeling the pinch, the lads that had opted for the mines were asking for a pay rise that was equivalent to my weekly wage, the greedy bastards were already on about £25 a week and now they were demanding another nine fucking quid.

The football was played in midweek during the afternoon, my kind hearted boss allowed me time off to enjoy a trip to Hillsborough.

Also during this period my dad's mother was not very well, she was living in those horrible flats on the Kelvin, after Hoyland Road had been raised to the ground.

He would go and spend the nights with her when the bloody lights went out, when I returned home from work all the street lights were out, the estate looked like a ghost town.

I opened the door and the house was like the black hole of Calcutta, all the family was huddled together in the kitchen, refugees because of the greedy miners.

Mum had got my tea ready, after I had finished it we all sat around the cooker trying to keep warm, it was bloody freezing outside.

Donna was perched in her high chair surveying the situation, Mum made sure that many candles illuminating the area, with no television to watch the compendium of games were brought out; we introduced the four year old David to the art of snakes and ladders.

With the old traditional coal fire lost forever, mum would provide the supper by toasting slice after slice of glorious toast, it was a poor substitute for the coal fired variety but it served the purpose, and mugs of piping hot cocoa were handed out.

Even when the lights came back on we would finish the evening off in that cosy kitchen before it was time for bed, these nights by the cooker ended soon after because the miners got what they wanted.

The £9 was reduced to £5 but it still was a 21% pay rise, they achieved another five days annual holiday and by 1974 the eighteen year olds would be on full pay.

Mind you it took them another nine days to return to work after they had brought the country and this city to its knees, and had cost the local steelworkers hundreds in lost wages including my dad.

Money that was hard to come by at the best of times, but never mind the greedy bastards didn't give a shit about anyone else.

I think most kids throughout the city got the piss taken out of them in one form or another, mechanics would be sent for the left handed spanners, while engineering firms would send the new starter for the long weight.

They would have them stood about for ages until the foreman or supervisor would tell them they had waited long enough.

Back on the money front I was trying to put some of my wages into my saving account but it was proving difficult to achieve, I was getting older and wanted to do more and more things.

I was fast approaching my seventeenth year, and the call of the nightclub was just around the corner. We had tried and failed miserably to gain entry to the Top Rank and finished up watching some erotic film at the Studio Five, Six and Seven in the Wicker, this was not how we wanted to spend our Saturday evenings.

The time was now right to try this club up in Nether Edge called Turn Ups. As we approached the dickie bow suited bouncer looked menacing. He must have known that we were only bits of kids but let us through. He must have been pissing himself outside because we were the only buggers in the place.

It was fucking empty, we purchased the drinks at sky high prices and looked for the darkest corner to hide our embarrassment. What time do these places fill up? It's ten thirty on a Saturday and there is four of us in the place.

I just felt like supping up and heading for the flea bitten cinema in the Wicker, but we stood our ground and in no time the place was buzzing; the sounds of the latest disco tunes were blaring out of the sound system.

This was it we had arrived, we were part of this suburban culture and we were strutting our funky stuff on the dance floor, mindful of the thousands of ladies handbags that littered the floor. What a night we had enjoyed.

Mind you it was a long walk back into town, we never stopped talking about it, I must have got home well after 4am, and I know one thing though I must have danced the alcohol out of my system because I was feeling ok.

Sunday morning I enjoyed the traditional breakfast before going out to kick the ball about. It was the summer months and we would just laze about on the school fields and listen to the transistor radio and envisage our next trip to the night club.

As we moved into 1973 I started to see less of my mates from the past five years, they had been there for me since I arrived on the estate in the summer of 1968, they started to mix more with their workmates and girls had also made an appearance.

At present I was single as single could be, I couldn't afford to finance myself at present so taking some bird to the pictures was well off my radar.

Mr Fiddler was spot on when he said that the kids you shared the classroom with, would drift away as you reached adulthood, we thought he was talking bollocks but he was now being proved right.

I think I had come through the past seventeen years relatively unscathed and enjoyed life to the full, like every story you hope for a happy ending. Well as I conclude this story I feel that this kid of steel has had many, many more ups than downs.

The Last of My Guardian Angels

The 16th of June 1972 and I am paying a fond farewell to the last of my guardian angels, it had now been over a decade that these three fine ladies had been fighting my corner, after my so called mother had beat a hasty retreat.

Looking back as one female departed my life, these Grandmothers came to the rescue, and Grandmothers was a fitting title, when I lost my Grandma Flo in 1968, it was a bitter pill to swallow.

She had been by my side for thirteen years, taking over the mantle was the loving Gertrude, after bringing up her own three children, she now had another three kids running around her block.

I was always disappearing when visiting the Manor, and loved kicking the ball about with the kids off the Manor, it was left to Mark and David to get into her hair, but this never troubled her, she never had a bad word to say against anyone.

Sadly though I never really got to know her, between 1966 and 1968 before we moved from the Shirecliffe to the Birley.

I rarely ventured to the Manor, I could never be located, so when my other two brothers were dragged across the city, I would find the sanctuary of the Shirecliffe tip rather more rewarding.

Her fingers must have been on fire because on their return I'd be the proud owner of a new knitted jumper in the most amazing colours that you could imagine.

On the odd occasion that I'd been tied to my mum's apron strings and made to travel over to the Manor, her three boys would all be jumpered up, the flannel would have been working overtime and how well we scrubbed up.

Whitsuntide and now I had another patch to fleece, dragging my two younger siblings around the Manor, street after street around Queen Mary Crescent would have been given the once over.

Our little pockets would be bulging; I don't think she took too kindly to us bringing the old Shirecliffe knock-knock across to Sheffield 2, could we be the next ultra-generation, bringing shame on ourselves, the family and worse of all, the entire Manor.

The words I used to love coming from her very polite lips was pass me my purse boys, I can hear the ice-cream man, and within minutes three lovely cornets would be lovingly passed onto us from her petite hands.

She was a very proud woman, her home was her palace, and she made lovely buns for us to eat; no fish dinner had been on her plates before she got onto making that lovely piping hot apple pie.

Flo and Gertrude were like chalk and cheese, both set in their ways, both independent, and both kept their husbands in check.

Sam always looked dapper and dressed like an Edwardian gentleman, he took a great pride in his appearance and so did his loving wife, they had been married for 33 years before Gertrude sadly passed away in 1970.

Another one of my guiding lights had been taken from me.

Along with Florence and William they were showing what could be achieved if you worked hard at your marital relationship, they too had been married 35 years until Florence died in 1968.

Florence Emily had outlived Granddad George Henry, that Arabian Knight had sadly departed in 1964, they had been together a mighty 43 years. They were showing the next generation how life together should be done, a total of 111 years of marital bliss between them, and a good part of that was spent dodging the bombs of old Adolf Hitler. After Hoyland Road had been razed to the ground, she found herself stuck in the so called streets in the sky that was the awful looking Kelvin Flats.

What a horrible place that was to visit, the flat was fine, but I felt the old lady was totally isolated.

No more ever again getting on her hands and knees and painstakingly returning her front step to its former glory with the old donkey stone, no more throwing her grandkids in that pot sink, and finally not having the cheating coalman deliver one sack short on his weekly delivery.

She must have been longing for those days to return, now she must have felt cheated, as she returned from shopping and had to manoeuvre up those piss stained stairs.

It was alright for the bastards from the council planning department, they did not have to suffer the fate of living in this shithole.

Gran's health started to suffer at an alarming rate, stuck in what can only be described as the largest pigeon loft in the world, but the pigeons had been replaced by the human population from the surrounding areas.

Dad would now finish his twelve hour shift driving his crane before heading to spend the night with his mother, before returning to work the following morning.

This he did for the final months of Gran's life, before she sadly passed away; this was 1972 so thankfully she had not had to endure many years living in the flats from hell.

Gran had not got any life insurance so it was down to the family to foot the bill, the funeral cortege left from 218 Portland Walk on the Kelvin, this included one hearse carrying dear old Gran and two sprays of flowers, while mum, dad, Grandad Sam were joined by Norma who was the daughter of William and Edith Harrison in the solitary funeral car.

I was at work while the kids were at school, while good old Auntie Shirley was looking after our Donna.

She was to be cremated at City Road Cemetery. On their arrival at Gran's final resting place; there to meet them was what can only be described as a gaggle of women.

It was Auntie Alice, Gertrude and Mary and the rest of the clan from Gran's side of the family, they had faces like thunder and their language was not one be fitting of the place they were attending.

It was more akin to some smoky dram shop in some back street boozer that language like theirs was more palatable.

Mum said their language was quite alarming for the place they were frequenting, sad really that you could count on two hands the number of people that were in attendance on this very sad day.

The lady who had seen enough in her 83 years, been war widowed at the age of 25 and left with a daughter to raise; given birth to my dad at the age of 42, and starting all over again in the maternal stakes, before looking after yours truly in 1962 at the age of 73, the girl had seen and done it all.

When the service was over, the gaggle turned their vile language onto my mum. What had she done to them? She hardly knew them, but the girl had no time to dwell she had three kids to sort out because it was nearing the end of the school day.

It later turned out that they were blaming mum for the break-up of the marriage of my so called birth mother; fucking hell, that girl was off long before their encounter in the Black Swan.

What was really bugging them was the fact that a public house had not been commissioned for the wake, and the chance of a free feast of ham and cheese sandwiches was not forthcoming while washed down with a couple of bottles of jubilee stout.

The funeral had cost a whopping great £85, did they not know that our family was struggling to make ends meet, and three school kids wanting feeding not the witches from Sheffield 5; their attitude really upset mum but she had no time to dwell on the matter, she had a more important engagement.

So that was it, the last of my guardian angels had gone forever, but I was now sixteen years of age, I had outgrown the pot sink, the outside lavatory, the need to be pushed around the Shirecliffe estate in my perambulator, the longing for very colourful knitwear, those extra arithmetic lessons down the cellar at number 112 Hoyland Road, those trips to Hillsborough and Longley Park, those days had sadly come to an end; but they were etched in my brain forever, and for that this kid of steel gives a heartfelt thank you to my three irreplaceable guardian angels.

About the author

Anthony Cronshaw was born on November 3, 1955, and attended Shirecliffe Infants and Junior School

When he was 11, his father remarried, to Marie and the family moved to the Birley Estate. For the first time in his life, Anthony had a real mother. His brothers, Mark and David, and sister Donna completed the family.